THE RECONCILIATION OF CHRIST AND NIETZSCHE

Understanding the Functional Organization and Structure of Philosophy

Dr. Charles T. Rowe

Copyright © 2004, Charles T. Rowe

ISBN: 0-9761007-0-3

LCCN: 2004096391

*Dedicated to our grandchildren's grandchildren
and their children and grandchildren*

CONTENTS

I	**INTRODUCTION**	1
	Three Seminal Questions	*1*
	Background and Starting Point	*2*
	Functional Definition of Ethical	*4*
	Two Themes Involved with Philosophy—	
	Individual and Group	*4*
	The Function of Philosophy	
	Outline of this Book	*5*
II	**THE STARTING ASSUMPTION**	9
	A Necessary Common Frame of Reference	
	Concept of Goals and Prioritization	*10*
	Subjective Goals	*11*
	Objective Goals	*12*
	Most Important Human Function vs.	
	Aristotle's Special Function	
	Other Objective Goals	*13*
	Self-preservation	
	Passing on our DNA	
	Preserving all Animals	
	Evolution—Worm to Ape to Man to Superman	
	Disagreement with Perpetuation of the Species	
	as most Important Function	*15*
	Russell's "Objective Truth"—	
	The Archimedean Point	*16*

III   **EPISTEMOLOGY AND LOGIC**   17
Data Acquisition and Processing

    Two Types of Data and Theories   18
        Objective for the Group
        Subjective for the Individual
        Improving Data and Theories

    Teleology and Truth   23
        Objective
        Subjective

    Appropriate Use of Objective by
    Group and Subjective by Individuals   24

IV   **ETHICS AND POLITICS**   27
What is the Ideal Way to Accomplish the Goal?

    Groups and their Rules   28
        Survival-of-the-Fittest
        Liberty vs. Equality
        Equality vs. Equal Opportunity
        All Humans are not of Equal Value
        Other Animals not Equal to Humans
        Kindness for and Limits on Sustaining
           the less Talented

    Description of an Ethical System   34
        Imbalances in Liberty vs. Equality—
           The Platonic Progression
        Democrats and Republicans

    Group Formation and Deontology   37
        Quid pro Quo–Protection for Increased
           Membership
        Ethical Pursuit of Happiness
        Additional Requirements
        Lack of Obligations to non-Group Members
        The Government Best that Governs Least
        Violation of the Contract—Unethical Behavior
        A Written Contract—The U.S. Constitution
        Breaking a Contract—The Declaration of
           Independence

      Defining the Parties that Assume the
          Obligations of the Contract

Intent of Conduct Irrelevant Regarding Ethical   47
    No Degrees of Good/Ethical
    Degrees of Unethical

The Advantages of Single-World-Group Theory   49
    Traditional Survival-of-the-Fittest Theory
    Why Strong Countries Need to Join a
        World Group
    Dealing with Outlying Groups

Problem of Religious based Groups   53
    Theocracies

Primary vs. Secondary Ethical Rules   55
    Ethical Rules do not Apply to All
    Reason, Awareness and Long-Term Planning

The Three Variables Involved   57
    Inductive Approach and Probabilities
    Broken Promises
    Preferred Deductive Approach to Ethics
    Ethical Egoism—An Oxymoron
    Inability to use Religion as Foundation
        for Ethics

The Necessity of Adjustable Ethics   63

V   ESTHETICS AND METAPHYSICS   65
    Why is man willing to do this job?

The Functional Definition of Esthetics   66
    Art and Artists

The Functional Definition of Metaphysics   68
    Metaphysics/Religion
    The Primacy of Ethics

Decadence   71
    Secular/Materialistic
    Religious/Maudistic
    Politics and Self-Indulgence

  Existentialism   74
   Opiate of the Masses
  Brief Review of the Completed Functional
   Structure of Philosophy   75

VI   UNDERSTANDING THE DIFFERENCE
   BETWEEN ETHICS AND MORALS   77
  Point-Counterpoint Chart   77
  Morals as Yesterday's Ethics   78
  Religion/Metaphysics and Morals   79
   As a Source of Unethical Behavior
  Relativism   81
  Moral Theories vs. Ethical Theories   83
   Justice as a Moral Theory–
    Rawls's A Theory of Justice
   Relevance of Intent
  Ethical Restrictions Imposed on Morals   87
  Usefulness of Ethical Theory Based on
   Perpetuation   88
   The Priority of Ethics over Morals

VII   THE JUDGMENTAL ROLE OF PHILOSOPHY   91
  Overloaded Lifeboat   91
  If only 200 from Earth can Survive   92
   Discourage use of Ethnic Designation in front of
    American
   Value of Virtues
  Ethical War   94
   Civilian Casualties
   When is War Ethical
   War as a Necessary Means
   Religion as Basis for War
   Secular Ethical Limits Imposed on War
    Massive Environmental Destruction
    Genocide as Crime against Humanity

Tribal Wars and Country Formation
Nonviolence and Ethics
Equality of Opportunity for Women   99
   Need for Protection
   Bearing and Raising Children
   Women and Men Ethically not Having Children
Slavery in America   103
   Unethical Inception
      Acceptance in Constitution—
         the Least Unethical of the Choices
   Proximate, Short-Term Unethical Results—
      Civil War
   Long-Term Unethical Sequelae
Suicide   110
   Depression
   End-of-Life
   Group Protection
   Ritual Suicide
Death Penalty   112
   Justice
Abortion and Population Control   113
   Resource Expense for Members Unable
      to Contribute
Environment   116
   Republicans and Environment—Democrats
      and War
   Global Warming
   Space Research and Exploration
Need for Single-World-Group   119
   Divisiveness of Religion
Perpetuation of the Species as an Ethical Theory   121

VIII POSTSCRIPT   123

   Popper's Comments Answered   123
   Answers to my Seminal Three Questions   124
   Acknowledgements and Observations   127

| IX | APPENDIX | 135 |

*Flow Chart of Structure and
   Organization of Philosophy* — *135*

*Obligations and Advantages of
   Deontological Contracts* — *136*

*Summary of Philosophy Based on Function and
   Perpetuation* — *138*

INTRODUCTION

"A scientist . . . can attack his problem straight away. He can go at once to the heart . . . of an organized structure . . . The philosopher finds himself in a different position. He does not face an organized structure, but rather something that resembles a heap of ruins.

Indeed, it has now become a recurrent question in philosophical circles whether philosophy will ever get so far as to pose a genuine problem."
— Karl Popper, *The Logic of Scientific Discovery,* Preface to the First Edition, 1934

I have always been fascinated by good questions. It has been this feature of my personality that set one domino falling into the next, leading me to organize my thoughts into this book. Over time, three questions for which I had not seen satisfying answers impelled me to formulate my own answers. The first was the question of how there could be reconciliation between the divergent philosophies of Nietzsche and Christ. The second came from a radio evangelist. In his presentation he posed the question of how could we know that the Holocaust was wrong if we did not have religion, in this case Christianity, and the *Bible*. The third question was from my wife. If there were only a single person, could he or she do anything that was unethical?

My academic training has been entirely in the biological and chemical disciplines needed to practice medicine plus the "once over lightly" studies at a liberal arts college 40 years ago. At that time, I neglected to take even an introductory course to philosophy. Curiously, that ignorance, that lack of background, is both an advantage and a hindrance. It has been an advantage, in that I have not been burdened by knowing what the answers or the approach should have been to address these questions. That same advantage is of course the hindrance, in that there can be excessive reinventing of the wheel and perhaps multiple important concepts that are never considered or poorly understood. Bernard Williams, in *Ethics and the Limits of Philosophy,* muses that some philosophers would like to go back and reflectively question our moral and ethical concerns without the weight of texts and philosophical study. While I may not have been a perfect philosophic tabula rasa, I definitely understood that remark. This writing is the product of such an unburdened approach.

Previously, my intellectual avocation was in history. The best I have read in this field was Will and Ariel Durant's *The Story of Civilization* and reading their masterwork provided me with some exposure to philosophy. In fact, when I started thinking about how to approach the subject, I began by looking up the definition of ethics in another of Will Durant's books, *The Story of Philosophy.* Here I found ethics defined as "the study of ideal conduct." The obvious question that followed was, "To accomplish what?" Most people who have had an exposure to philosophy have an answer to that question since it has been asked and answered for at least 2300 years. I, however, was not burdened by any of the already known "correct" answers. Coming from a much more biologic bent, the obvious answer to me was, and is, *"perpetuation of the species."* That is to say, human beings' most important job, our most important function, is that of survival as a species. Whatever else our conduct might hope to accomplish, our ideal conduct must first ensure our perpetuation. This then raises a basic point in answering any question or reading someone else's answers. Be very aware and wary of what the starting point is, for it is this critical first assumption from which all else follows. If you do not agree with the basic starting point then don't get too excited about the rest of the discussion.

The starting point must be a common frame of reference, the sine qua non required to begin any discussion, for otherwise we have apples versus oranges arguments with no way to adjudicate the conflicting opinions and disputes. It is my assumption that the conduct philosophy recommends is to apply to all of us—humanity as a whole—and it is therefore my further presumption that this necessary starting point must be objective so that it can be clearly understandable to all members of humanity involved in the discussion. Subjective starting points can be couched in many terms, but, from intuitive to divine, they all represent personal and individual values and opinions. Personal opinion, no matter how fervent, does not translate into consistent group agreement. Any subjective starting point is likely to have as many different nuances as there are people in the world at that given time. Thus, any subjective starting point is unusable for the base needed to produce consensus for the study of philosophy and life's conduct. If, however, we can agree on an objective basis for beginning our discussion, then this well-recognized objection is not applicable.

My contention in this presentation is that most humans, upon reflection and after considering the alternatives, will agree that nothing is more important than the long-term survival of human beings, perpetuation of the species. To those who would say that their family, ethnic or tribal group, country, etc. is more important than the rest of humanity, suffice it to agree for the moment that any concept of individual existence is less important than survival of some group, some part of humanity beyond one's self. It will be discussed later how this more limited concept of perpetuation of one's family or other subgroup fits into the larger concept of perpetuation of the species.

This contention will be my starting point. The "greatest good" will be defined as "perpetuation of the species." It will be used as the most important goal or end for humanity. Lack of agreement is unfathomable to me since disagreement would necessarily imply that the contrarian would sacrifice all of humanity for some alternate personal temporary existence or subjective opinion. It sounds idealistically nice for Kant to say that life without justice is not worth living—but do you really believe that? Without life there isn't even the concept of justice! If there is no life, there will be no concerns about the meaning of life. Issues that seem critical to us as individuals, such as justice or even afterlife, become moot points that our never-born descendants will have no opportunity to consider if we cannot perpetuate our species.

Using this starting point, the elements of philosophy will be shown as forming an organized structure with each of the elements performing a necessary function in order to give human beings the best chance of long-term survival. It is a look at the whole elephant, philosophy, through the lens of survival of the species. It is my intent in the course of this writing to address the two problems posed by Karl Popper quoted at the start of this introduction. My object is to demonstrate an organized structure of philosophy, to show how the elements work together and how opinions or concepts fit into this whole. Using this organizational structure, judgments as to right or wrong can then be considered objectively. This concept demands that all points of view must be held to the standard of do they or don't they contribute to the long-term top priority of survival of the species. This demand becomes the definition of ethical or unethical conduct for the group—ethical conduct is conduct that gives humanity the best chance of perpetuation of the species; unethical conduct is that which is detrimental to the goal of perpetuation. We can also see in this definition that a functional approach to philosophy works more with what philosophy and its component parts do rather than what they are. Ethics *is* ideal conduct or the study of ideal conduct. What ethics functionally *does* is to guide us in the best way to avoid extinction, and it, thus, considers results rather than intent or idealism.

Philosophy, with its functional structure, is, of course, about how we humans deal with life. There are two interwoven themes. The theme of primary importance is that of perpetuation of the group of humans as a whole. The secondary theme is how each individual plays his or her temporary role in the long-running production of human existence. The point counterpoint is the survival of humanity over time versus the desire for happiness of the ephemeral individual. The function of philosophy can thus be seen as the integration of the prioritized objective needs of the group for long-term survival with the vital but secondarily important desires of the individual for happiness during his or her relatively brief lifetime.

Following this introduction, the next section will deal with selection of the starting assumption, the common frame of reference. After the starting assumption, there is an almost overwhelming urge to start on ethics, following a life is short—eat dessert first philosophy. However, Confucius' advice—knowledge must come before action—is apt and we must next discuss how we gather data and process it—epistemology and logic—in order to decide what conduct to recommend. In keeping with our group versus individual themes and using our functional approach, it will be seen there are two types of data—objective and subjective. The group will try to use only objective data while the individual feels free to also use subjective data. With these data, predictive theories are formed and from these theories come philosophy's recommendation for ideal conduct. The fourth section then deals with this ideal conduct—ethics and politics. Perpetuation of the species—the theme of primary importance—is a group function. Ethics is the rules and politics the mechanism for formulating and applying the rules for the group. Realizing that liberty means few restraints, hence, few rules, and that equality requires many restraints and, hence, many rules, the discussion turns to how the process of ethics and politics is a balancing act of managing the reciprocal values of liberty and equality. The purpose of these rules is first and foremost to assure us that the human race will survive; and if done optimally, the rules, our ethics, will give us the best chance of getting this job done.

The fifth section deals with esthetics and metaphysics. This is the realm of the individual. This is the area of philosophy that rewards us individually for doing the job that ethics requires of us. Our salary for doing this job is our individual, subjective reward of happiness. We can find our happiness either in the natural world or in subjective thoughts regarding the supernatural world. Our own thoughts and desires, our own pursuit of happiness in this world or another, are ours and cannot be ethically denied *unless our individual pursuit of happiness in whatever action compromises the ability of the group to accomplish the group goal of perpetuation.* It is in this restriction where we understand that the group's needs come first in order to ensure perpetuation of the species. Here is the tricky part of philosophy—the requirement that an individual's pursuit of happiness, including religion, be subordinated to the more important group goal. Each of our individual values and desires comes second to the need of perpetuation of the group.

That leads to our sixth section—understanding the difference between ethics for the group and morals of the individual. While usually these two areas have much in common, it is when the differences occur that we encounter virtually all of the ethical dichotomies. Most of these, if not all, are the result of situations in which our personal values tell us one thing but the ethical needs of the group require another choice. It is important to realize that these conundrums are really two questions in one, and that the group's ethics has priority over the individual's morals.

The last section deals with the judgmental role of philosophy. With the structure of the elements of philosophy in place, some of the traditional problems of philosophy are examined. Using the objective goal that is the premise of this book, a different form of utilitarianism is apparent. The end really does justify the means; all actions are means, e.g., both war and peace; and philosophy's assignment is to decide when each is appropriate given the circumstances, resources and threats. Since the goal is objective and decisions must be based on reality, it ensues that most of us will be disappointed at some of the necessary actions ethics requires. Would that it could be some other way, but nobody ever said the job would be easy.

At the end of the book is a postscript with credits, some observations on philosophic approaches in general, and some opinions I developed in the course of thinking about a functional approach to philosophy. The postscript also gives my answers to the seminal three questions stated in the first paragraph.

The real key is the starting assumption. There is nothing more important to human beings than ensuring perpetuation of the species. Death of the individual is inevitable. It will, however, be taken as a given, the common frame of reference, that nonsurvival of the race as a whole is ipso facto unethical and on that rock will be built the structure and function of philosophy. To give ourselves the best chance of accomplishing this end we will justify our ethics, and ethics is after all the end product of philosophy.

THE STARTING ASSUMPTION

A NECESSARY COMMON FRAME OF REFERENCE

> "Some . . . say: 'I do not know what is meant by 'objective truth,' but I shall consider a statement 'true' if all, or virtually all, of those who have investigated it are agreed in upholding it.' . . . We are then faced with a question of fact: are there any similarly agreed statements in ethics? If there are, they can be made the basis both for rules of private conduct, and for a theory of politics . . . If there are not, we are driven in practice . . . to a contest by force or propaganda or both, whenever an irreconcilable ethical difference exists between powerful groups."
> —Bertrand Russell *A History of Western Philosophy*

> " . . . for the origin seems to be more than half the whole, and makes evident the answer to many of our questions . . . , perhaps we shall find the best good if we first find the function of a human being."
> —Aristotle's *Nicomachean Ethics*

> "I think everyone should love life above everything in the world. Love life more than the meaning of it? Certainly, . . ."
> —Alyosha from *The Brothers Karamazov* by Fyodor Dostoyevsky

If ethics is the study of ideal conduct, then what is that conduct to accomplish? It is a question that, not surprisingly, was considered by Aristotle 2300 years ago. What is the "good" at which everything aims? What is the goal, the desired end? In the hierarchy of goods what is the most important good—the greatest good—to which all others must be subordinate? We must start with our human mission statement. This defines the primary job (goal, end, etc.), the job with the top priority, the one job that must be accomplished even if no other human jobs get done. The selection of this job will define ethics—the code of ideal conduct used to get this job done. As Aristotle phrased it, " . . . in every action and decision it is the end, since it is for the sake of the end that everyone does the other things."

There is another possible approach to life and ideal conduct. This approach would say there is no goal for life and humans have no particular job to do. In this scenario, anything goes. There would be no need for ethics, no ideal conduct, no need to consider any other aspects of life. Any final product of life, any end, is as acceptable as any other. If you have no goal you can't be disappointed. Any conduct will work. "Is it just for the moment we live?" If you agree with this approach, that there is no goal or end to life, then the answer to the question from Bacharach's song is, yes, it is only for the moment and any conduct is acceptable. Fortunately for those of us here in this generation, this is not how most humans have operated throughout history.

There is a similar problem with any system that has ill-defined or multiple possible goals. If your goal is not clearly defined then how do you know if you have achieved it? The primary goal has to be specifically articulated since that is the result, more than all of the other possibilities, you will strive to make happen. Some, rather than thinking in terms of goals, would place their top priority on the conduct itself—the means. Usually this entails being nice, using variants of the golden rule or the virtues. The consequences of this means-determines-the-ends approach would be a number of possible results, a "realm" of possible goals. Presumably, long-term human survival would be one of the possibilities in this realm, but if it is not the top priority then inevitably decisions will be made that will not give humanity the best chance of perpetuation. If perpetuation is the agreed-upon goal then this end must determine the means and not the other way around. There can be secondary goals including being nice, but the primary goal always takes precedence. Any and all secondary goals, any and all means must be abandoned if not doing so would jeopardize the primary goal. If any goal other than perpetuation of the species is chosen, then at best perpetuation of the species becomes a secondary priority in such a system and can be sacrificed in order to ensure that the alternate top priority is attained. One has to ask if losing humanity could possibly be less important than any other priority. I think, I hope, that we can collectively agree that perpetuation is our most important goal—our highest and greatest good. Let me review it a bit more systematically.

Most of us are, I believe, willing to consider that humanity has an Aristotelian hierarchy of "goods" and that there is a top priority for our lives. Selections for our designated primary human job, our top priority, can come from either of two categories: one category chooses from options in the subjective and/or supernatural world; the other chooses from options in the natural, secular, objective world.

Options from the subjective category include religion, happiness, and intuitive values. Ethical systems that seem benevolent and appealing can be described using these options, but since the goals of these systems are subjective, and possibly supernatural, there is no way for humanity as a group to have a unified concept of what they entail. None of them can provide the common frame of reference absolutely necessary if we as a human group are to agree on recommended conduct. It is this inability to provide a common frame of reference that is the inescapable Achilles' heel of all ethical systems founded on a subjective basis. The logical positivists are well known for this type of argument. Bertrand Russell, among others, pointed out that an individual's values cannot be intellectually confirmed nor can they be proved incorrect (see verifiable and falsifiable under the section on epistemology and logic) and therefore cannot represent a point of objective, general agreement. One cannot start with a subjective, nonverifiable basis and expect to get objective, verifiable conclusions. This does not stop groups of individuals who think they agree on a subjective option from assuming a subjective starting point and proceeding from there. It is important to recognize, however, that with this approach the number of starting points is limitless and variations in understanding the starting points will vary widely. Therefore, the ideal conduct to accomplish subjective goals will also vary widely. Thus, subjective approaches will result in limitless numbers of groups of individuals, each with its own rules of conduct for accomplishing their own individual goals, but subjective approaches offer no reasonable chances of general agreement as to how humanity as a whole should approach philosophy and conduct. The other possible approaches consider options from the objective, secular category.

I have long held a personal theory that good questions are harder to come by than good answers. In fact, good questions often lead to obvious answers to what at first seem to be complicated problems. To ask, "What is the function of a human being?" is a good question, but Aristotle (and philosophy in general) got off the track, refining the question to, "What is the *special* function of human beings?" The problem is better brought into focus by asking, "What is the most important function of human beings?" Still better, and more clearly focused, is to consider the reverse of the question. "What is the one function, if not accomplished, that would be the most disastrous for human beings?" The obvious answer to this question is perpetuation of human beings. We lose it all if we fail to perpetuate the species of man. Thus, the one function above all others that is the most important is perpetuation of our species—the avoidance of extinction. This is the exact same function that we humans assign to every other animal species, but we forget to then look in the mirror. Any species, including Homo sapiens, may exist for millennia or even millions of years but it may disappear only once.

Perhaps it is a disappointment for humans, with our large quota of hubris, to realize that in this function we have the same priority as plants and oxen and every *other* animal. Whatever the peculiar special attributes that specify our niche in the animal kingdom, we are no less animals than horses or mice, and the primary function of mice and men is the same. The distracting question our individual egos want to try to answer for ethics is, "What is our special function apart from other animals?" In its place, that too is a good question, but that place is found in the answers to what gives man happiness, and that in turn is dealt with appropriately in esthetics and metaphysics not ethics. Trying to substitute answers for human beings' special function for an answer to human beings' most important function is a fundamental error in defining ethical conduct.

There are other possible answers from the category of the natural, objective world in addition to perpetuation of the species. These include self-preservation, passing on our DNA, preservation of all life forms, and evolution to a higher order or species. Spinoza's self-preservation as the foundation of all virtue (Baruch Spinoza, *The Ethics of Spinoza*) is too narrow to be the basis for ethics. Self-preservation is the basis for individual happiness. Any one individual life is not as important as the life of the group as a whole, particularly since we each recognize that self-preservation is limited to one lifetime. This does not mean we each do not value our own lives. Rather it means, for almost all of us, we would agree that our personal, temporary existence is less important than the survival of our family, town, country or the whole of the human race. Most of us acknowledge that there are ideals and goals worth dying for. Parents would do so for their children. Soldiers in every generation do so for their country. Considering self-preservation brings into focus one of the fundamental issues of philosophy: the most important function is a group goal, not an individual goal. No individual alone can accomplish perpetuation. Self-preservation alone gains nothing in the long run. It is good to understand this fact since ethics will prove to be a group problem with a group goal and not an individual problem with an individual goal. It is true that some of us have to survive, but any one of us is expendable and each of us will certainly die. At best self-preservation lasts for only one generation.

There is a similar problem if we try to base ethics on the concept of passing on our DNA. This also is too limited in scope. Clearly this aspect of preservation of the species is vital in a general sense. However, it is too limiting in that one can pass on one's DNA without ensuring that the species will survive. Having a child does not ensure that the child will survive or that resources have been maintained to enable the child to continue the species into the future. One night in bed or rape in the bushes may succeed in passing on DNA once, but not indefinitely. A broader scope is needed. There are multiple other ways to achieve extinction besides not passing on your DNA. The goal for ethics must consider all of them.

Some believe that man is just another animal undeserving of a preferred position above all the other animals. Indeed, all the other species are working hard to preserve their species, just as man does. However, if the most important goal is perpetuation of our species, then it is more important to preserve the species man over other species. If one believes it is no more important man should survive rather than, for example, cats, then this alternative option can be used as your basis. There is no question, however, that this alternative basis will not have consensus and will not provide the necessary common frame of reference. In a system based on all species having equal rights, an acceptable goal could result in the elimination of humans while preserving more of other species. Eliminating our collective grandchildren's grandchildren to preserve other species is not acceptable to me. Thus, equalizing all species is not acceptable to me, and nor do I believe it would be acceptable to most humans as a primary assumption. There are secondary reasons that fit in with my primary goal of why I do want to preserve other species, but since I have to choose one supremely important primary goal, I choose to preserve the human species over all others. Equal rights of all species is not acceptable since it could compromise this primary goal.

The last alternative, objective possibility to be considered assumes that man in current form is a stepping-stone in a continuum of evolution, as Nietzsche phrased it–from worm to ape to man to superman. Nietzsche later denied that he meant to imply any further evolutionary product other than man himself. Still, I like his imagery: the problem is in knowing what man is supposed to be evolving into. If that is not known, then how can we plan our existence to make it happen? Maybe we will start planning for strong people, only to find in the next generation that what we really need are smart people. Or maybe neither plan is what will be most needed. Maybe what we will most need is people who are resistant to germs not yet encountered. It is unknown if the species of Homo sapiens will modify and evolve to a different species. If it happens, it will depend on the threats we encounter. Since those threats are, at best, uncertain, we cannot use this concept to formulate a basic assumption to deal with philosophy today. This evolutionary thought is worthwhile, however, for the humbling effect it should have on man's ever-present arrogance.

Not all will agree that perpetuation of the species is the most important goal even from among the objective category of options. In my estimation these outliers will fall roughly into three groups. The first of these will be the egotists who really do think their short-term existence is somehow more important than their family, village or country. I believe this sociopathic group represents a very small percentage of humans. The second group includes those who truly believe that other animals have the same ethical status as humans. Most of us like dogs or cats or horses or birds or camels or other animals, and often we see an important role for animals in our personal lives. We also see an important role for other animals in the necessary preservation of our environment. These observations, however, should not be taken as granting equal status to other animal species. I believe that the overwhelming majority of us would choose to prevent the extinction of man even if the only way it could be done forced the extinction of other animal species.

The third category includes those who will agree to preserve and perpetuate their tribe, family, country or ethnic group, but not humanity as a whole species. Preserving one's ethnic, tribal or national group in preference to others is biologically recognized as survival-of-the-fittest. Throughout history this has been an effective way to perpetuate the species. The history of man is entirely consistent with man operating under the survival-of-the-fittest theory. This theory requires no particular awareness on the part of the participants that it is being followed. The animal man holds this theory in common with many other animal species as being the best way to preserve the species. It is consistent with preservation of the species as the most important function of human beings and is not a problem with the basic assumption. Later, I will argue that humans should be in the process of replacing this theory with a better single-world-group theory. The transition is, however, incomplete. Still, this category of survival-of-the-fittest is not in disagreement with the perpetuation premise but is merely a specific approach used to accomplish perpetuation of the species.

More problematic than those not agreeing among the objective possibilities are those individuals who would select their subjective, often religious, goal as most important. As I noted earlier, this will result in multiple groups of individuals each with a different goal, adjusting their conduct accordingly. Some of these approaches will be benign and may integrate effectively within a larger group with a goal of perpetuation. After all, most, even among the strongly religious, would choose to preserve their children and grandchildren rather than eliminate them in a religiously inspired mass suicide such as occurred at Jonestown. Still, Jonestown provides a useful example that this thinking does not apply to all in this subjective area. A major danger of using the subjective approach for a primary goal is that some groups of individuals may develop goals antithetical to perpetuation of the species. Such goals could pose an ethical threat not only to themselves but also possibly to the rest of humanity. In fact, it is all too possible that a religiously inspired mass suicide plan could involve nuclear explosives in a worldwide Gotterdammerung rather than a limited poisoning of individuals. Thus, in addition to subjective goals being unable to provide a verifiable common frame of reference, they may have a decidedly negative, unethical impact on those with the objective goal of perpetuation of the species.

So, we have our common frame of reference, our Archimedean point. Human beings' most important function, the goal, is perpetuation of the human species. It is this that will be used (from the quote at the start of this section) as Russell's "objective truth." It is this that can be made "the basis both for rules of private conduct, and for a theory of politics." It is basic, so basic that if we fail to accomplish this goal, this greatest good, then the other goals for humans become moot points. Defining our most important function, and using it as the goal, gives the answer to the second portion of Karl Popper's quote cited at the start of the Introduction. The genuine problem posed by philosophy is, "How do we accomplish perpetuation of the human species?" Philosophy is not a collection of separate entities resembling a "heap of ruins"—the concern noted in the first part of Popper's quote. The elements of philosophy form an organized structure that enables us to develop answers to this basic question. The foundation of this functional structure of philosophy is built on data and theories, and so we next consider epistemology and logic.

EPISTEMOLOGY AND LOGIC

DATA ACQUISITION AND PROCESSING

"Maybe there are people who can act without knowledge, but I am not one of them. Hear much, pick the best and follow it . . ."
—The Analects of Confucius translation by Simon Leys

"Remember that to change thy opinion and to follow him who corrects thy error is as consistent with freedom as it is to persist in thy error"
—The Meditations of Marcus Aurelius

"A centipede was happy quite
Until a frog in fun
Said, 'Pray which leg comes after which?'
This raised her mind to such a pitch,
She lay distracted in a ditch
Considering how to run."
—Unknown Author

The dictionary definition of epistemology is the branch of philosophy that studies the nature of knowledge, its presupposition and foundations, and its extent and validity. The dictionary definition of logic is the study of the principles of reasoning, especially of the structure of propositions as distinguished from their content and of method and validity in deductive reasoning. Functionally, epistemology and logic provide the organized structure of philosophy with data acquisition and processing. We have a goal, a job to do, and we must first gather the information that tells us how to approach this job. Basic statements, singular existential statements, initial conditions, atoms, elementary propositions are all terms that have been used to semantically describe the data. The basic data are processed into theories. These theories are the final functional product of this first category of philosophy comprised of epistemology and logic. These two form the base from which all else in philosophy follows. We humans then work with these theories to make decisions regarding how to live and conduct ourselves. The above three opening quotes summarize the process. We get the best information we can, and we conduct ourselves accordingly. If better information and theories become available then we change our conduct. Sophist arguments about the complete accuracy of even objective data may be interesting, but we cannot let them keep us from making decisions. We do not have the luxury of "lying in a ditch, considering how to run." We must use the best data and theories we have and keep on running.

Functionally the data we use fall into two general categories: objective and subjective. Objective data can be defined as data that can be verified by knowledgeable, disinterested members of the human group. Because unbiased group members can verify these data, they can be used for further processing by the group as a whole. Subjective data are those data that can be verified only by the individual. These data are therefore not useable by the group as a whole.

It is the group as a whole that must continue to solve the basic problem of life and philosophy—perpetuating the species. No individual alone can perpetuate the species. For maximum likelihood of success, the whole group must work towards the group solution of this problem. This requires group acceptable data to be used in order that all or most of the group can understand and agree on the approach to the solution. Without some level of uniformity in understanding and agreement, the group could not work cohesively and efficiently toward the goal. Minor disagreement in acceptable data results in group inefficiency with some strain on cohesiveness. Extensive disagreement results in dissolution of the group. Therefore, the group must form the needed theories using only objective data so as to assure maximum efficiency. These theories will describe the best conduct for the group, the conduct that will give the group the best chance of perpetuation.

Given its crucial role in solving this real world objective problem, recommended conduct cannot afford to rely on subjective data or individual values or opinions. Objective data are processed into cause and effect associations with theories formulated to be predictive for natural events. Objective theories are characterized by being testable and objectively able to be confirmed. An even more important attribute, according to Popper, is that they can potentially be falsified. No theory can ever be completely verified but it must be testable—able to be tested with results that confirm the theory, provisionally verify it, or prove it incorrect, falsify it. Objective theories must be accepted by knowledgeable, disinterested members of the group. Testability is the sine qua non of this requirement. These testable objective theories provide the basis for group acceptable theories of conduct. This conduct is ethics.

It is understood that the process of gathering objective data, cause and effect postulating and forming theories is never perfect. That is the nature of the real world—the nature of nature. The process depends on recording data that will continue to be refined and on formulating theories that can be falsified and therefore need improvement. It is a system based on probabilities. As data improve, the theories improve and cause and effect is better understood. All of the objective data and theories in the Newtonian macro world are in turn based on quantum data in the micro world where the uncertainty principle is a basic foundation. It would seem that, Einstein notwithstanding, nature/god in the micro world does roll dice The important point for epistemology and logic is that imperfection is no excuse for inaction. While data, and therefore theories, will never be perfect, knowledgeable, disinterested members of the group must still formulate theories and conduct based on the best data available and the highest probability that the resulting predictions will give the group the best possible chance for perpetuation. The best and fittest of the available group-accepted theories become the necessary working theories for the group used to determine conduct. When better objective data come along then the theories change.

The second category of data is subjective. These are data that individuals choose to use for their personal happiness, particularly religious data. These data do not have to be verifiable by the group at large and may be used by any number of individuals or even a group of individuals, but only for their individual purposes. Since subjective data are unable to be confirmed or accepted by the group as a whole, these data are not usable by the group as a whole. Hence, theories developed from these subjective data cannot be used by the group as a whole. Since it is the group that is involved with ethics, subjective data and resultant theories cannot form any group consensus basis for ethics.

Still, there is an important role for subjective data and theories. So long as they do not affect the goal of perpetuation of the group as a whole, an individual can use any data and theories he or she wants, in order to seek personal, individual happiness. Those data can be objective or subjective. Even the subjective data can have meaning for an individual even if the group at large doesn't agree with them. It is not correct to say that the statement "There is a God" is meaningless. Rather, it is correct to say that this statement is subjective and as such it is not usable to the group of humans as a whole in establishing rules to accomplish the primary job. However, it is also correct to say that this statement has considerable meaning for some individuals. For them, this subjective data can be used to construct an important subjective theory. It is thus a useful, even vital, statement when applied to the appropriate category of individual esthetics and happiness. At the same time, it is divisive and detrimental when attempts are made for such an individual subjective concept to be used to create the rules/ethics needed for the whole group to accomplish an objective primary goal.

The functional terms, objective and subjective, provide the demarcation needed to accommodate the basic division of philosophy into the group's problem of ethics and the individual's problem of happiness. Functionally, it is unimportant whether such things as Einstein's equations, string theory or black holes could be defined as empirical knowledge. What is important is whether knowledgeable, disinterested members of the group agree that they are correct. If so, they can be accepted as objective and can be used by the group to develop ethical theories.

It is recognized that, historically, there have been data accepted as objective that are no longer in that category. For example, in the past, the existence of God is a concept that has been accepted as objective. However, after the last century, with the introduction and recognition of the requirements of testable, verifiable and falsifiable, this concept is, today, extremely unlikely to be accepted as objective by knowledgeable, disinterested members of the now larger world group. For God, as an ethically useful concept, to be accepted as objective would require, for example, a uniform understanding and agreement from China, India, Iran and Spain. Such acceptance is not even remotely likely. Even in America, with the now more diverse background of its members, there is no agreement among disinterested individuals. This concept is, therefore, now considered subjective and no longer usable by the group to develop ethical theories. Individuals can, of course, still use this subjective concept to develop esthetic and metaphysical theories dealing with individual happiness.

Our basic usable data originated with and are still dependent on man's basic senses. Today, in addition to innate sensory input, man has expanded this database to include better more precise receptors such as telescopes, microscopes, better recording devices, and instruments capable of sampling much more of the electromagnetic spectrum rather than the restricted bandwidth available to the human eye. As receiving and recording devices continue to improve, the information they provide will continue to be better. Then, the process as a whole, further extended by better reasoning and theory formulation, will improve. Regardless, at any given time, man must use the data available and process it, as best he can, to form the best explanations of how the universe and our small part of it, the earth, works. The information will never be perfect and will always be better in the future. Still, this does not absolve us from trying to accomplish the primary job as best that we can. Playing the part of the frog in our opening quote can be helpful if it puts us on the right track for understanding problems and solving problems. However, we do not have the luxury of the centipede "lying in a ditch considering how to run." Likewise we do not have the luxury of purposeful sophistry to try and keep the centipede from doing what needs to be done. We use our objective data to build the best theories we can at the time, using the best processes for theory building that we have available. These theories are then used by the group to formulate conduct needed to accomplish the group goal. In Karl Popper's words, there is an "urgency of replacing a falsified hypothesis by a better one . . . We choose the theory which best holds its own in competition with other theories; the one which, by natural selection, proves itself fittest to survive." It is expected and unavoidable that data will improve, the database will expand, conditions will change, and the environment will change. All theories, in all likelihood, will be either replaced or improved. They will change. Regardless, we use the best we have at the time and move on when we have better data and theories.

The breakdown into objective and subjective does leave a "gray" zone. This is the area where the data and theories are ostensibly objective but not yet accepted by the group as a whole. Practically speaking, until the group is able to accept them, they cannot be used. They can be proposed but not yet applied. A major cause for this circumstance is inertia, where the group will adhere to older long-used theories in preference to new ones. The reluctance to accept new theories may have benefits by keeping some stability in the group and by keeping new theories that are less fit or eventually proved wrong out of the mainstream. There is a practical usefulness to the maxim "if it ain't broke, don't fix it." The downside of this reluctance to change is, of course, that ignoring a new theory that works better diminishes the group's ability to attain its primary goal. New objective theories can and must be tested and shown to the group's satisfaction to be better than what is currently in use. When it is objectively shown that the new theory is better, then it is unethical not to change. We must keep in mind that this property of testability, emphasized by Popper, in the final analysis, is what will separate objective from subjective. Personal values, beliefs, faiths are subjective and as such are not testable by the group and, therefore, will not be acceptable for the group as a whole. If what is not testable today becomes observable and testable tomorrow, then we test it, change our opinion and move it into the objective category where it can then be used in developing group accepted theories. Conversely, there are also data and theories that have been accepted as objective in the past that, with the advent of better data and better theories, have been shown false. Still others, such as those based on intuitive or a priori data, previously accepted become unusable in the objective category because of the relatively recent recognition of the requirement of testability.

In epistemology and logic, the search for the "Holy Grail," the ultimate theory, is the search for a theory that is perfect in its ability to predict events. This corresponds to the study of teleology, the search for knowledge of the perfect, or ultimate, end of the human process. There are two different routes, objective and subjective, for the study of teleology. The objective route, for use by the group, will never have absolute certainty. This route must deal with objective theories that can be tested and falsified. Objective theories deal only in probabilities. There can be no absolute "truth" in the objective world. The alternative route is the individual subjective approach. This does not require testability. Each individual can subjectively decide for himself or herself what the ultimate end will be and need not convince any other member of the group. The subjective theory of the ultimate end of the human process needs to be perfectly correct only in the one individual's mind. Hence, subjective theories, most notably religious theories, can be translated into "truth" for the individual.

The search for the ultimate objective theory deals with objective cosmological questions regarding the fate of the universe: Is it a virtual particle that will blink out in a black hole? Will it continue to expand? Is it a process of repeated expansion and contraction? etc. The ultimate subjective theories can choose to deal with supernatural religious theories or other subjective, intuitive, a priori theories that cannot be tested and, hence, cannot be proved wrong. The virtue of the subjective approach is that multiple theories can provide "truth" and ultimate answers for individuals. However, these multiple answers will not work for the group as a whole. It is important to understand that untestable, unfalsifiable, a priori, intuitive and other subjective data are not infallible truth in the objective category. Herein lies a fundamental danger for humanity—the overwhelming desire that each of the millions of us has to impose our subjective, individual version of "truth" on the group as a whole, even when this imposition might be detrimental to the objective goal of perpetuation of the group.

Thus we see the necessary product that is derived from epistemology and logic. This process provides the predictive theories needed for the group and for individuals to make decisions about conduct. The group requires objective data processed to yield testable theories, which then result in theories that describe rules that we call ethics—the conduct that the group should follow if it is to give itself the best chance for perpetuation. In addition, the individual can, and often does, use subjective data to formulate additional theories of benefit and value to the individual. The objective rules will be dealt with in depth in the section on ethics and politics. Subjective concepts and theories will be dealt with in the section on esthetics and metaphysics. Still, even at this early juncture, we can see that the objective theories for accomplishing the primary goal, by definition the group's most important, take precedence over the subjective theories that fulfill individual desires. Thus we start to examine and balance our two intertwined themes—the needs of the group versus the desires of the individual. We now understand that anything an individual does that makes it less likely that the group can accomplish its primary goal is, by definition, unethical. Thus, in the area of epistemology and logic, purposefully falsifying data is unethical. Likewise, trying to substitute a subjective theory for an objective theory is unethical. Hence, for example, trying to replace an objective theory of evolution with a subjective creationist theory is unethical. If individuals subvert the objective process with bad data or subjective data, then the group has decreased its ability to make decisions regarding the best conduct needed for perpetuation in the objective, natural, secular world. With an objective goal, the group must deal with the best objective data and theories available. Any attempt to dilute that data or those theories with personal, subjective, "infallible truth" is unethical.

Epistemology and logic function to provide us with ever better information, which enables us to formulate predictive theories to recommend conduct. These two elements provide the foundation on which the rest of philosophy is built. With this foundation in place, we next consider the rules developed from objective theories that describe the conduct needed by the group. This conduct is our ethics. The development, application and administration of the rules of conduct for the group constitute politics. Our next section will thus consider these—ethics and politics.

ETHICS AND POLITICS

WHAT IS THE IDEAL WAY TO ACCOMPLISH THE GOAL?

"... in everything one must consider the end ..."
—A favorite quote of John Adams
from *John Adams* by David McCullough

"Always, then, acts are called good or bad, according as they are well or ill adjusted to ends; and whatever inconsistency there is in our uses of the words, arises from inconsistency of the ends."
—Herbert Spencer, *The Principles of Ethics*

"What, then, is the good in each of these cases? Surely it is that for the sake of which the other things are done; and in medicine this is health, in generalship victory, in housebuilding a house, in another case something else, but in every action and decision it is the end, since it is for the sake of the end that everyone does the other things."
—Aristotle, *Nicomachean Ethics,*
translated by Terence Irwin

Using perpetuation of the species as the most important human function—the function that we can least afford to not accomplish—provides the necessary goal or end noted in the quotes above. It also provides us with a necessary common frame of reference. As noted, some individuals and groups of individuals will not agree. Still, I am positing that, on reflection, a significant majority of humanity will agree that long-term human survival—perpetuation—is the most important function and can serve as humanity's agreed upon objective goal. Acquiring data and formulating theories develop the rules for achieving this goal of the group. The set of developed rules, referred to by such terms as laws, contracts or commandments, describe the conduct for accomplishing this goal. This, then, constitutes the ethics for that group. I will also consider the implications of groups with alternative goals since this lack of agreement with the majority has to be considered and accounted for in determining ethics.

Later, I will propose an objective theory, that humanity would be better able to perpetuate itself and the various groups within the world by operating as a single world group. However, this opening discussion of ethics will consider groups in a generic fashion, more in keeping with how world groups have operated historically—survival-of-the-fittest. The functional definition of survival-of-the-fittest is as follows: any group, smaller than the group of world humanity, that considers itself so important that, if necessary for it to survive, would eliminate or permit elimination of all other groups. As noted earlier in the Starting Assumption, survival-of-the-fittest is an important method used by many members of the animal kingdom to perpetuate species. It requires no awareness of any big picture or overall plan to function effectively. Historical facts support the premise that human groups have had as their primary goal perpetuation of their own group. In so doing, they have worked under the survival-of–the-fittest theory of perpetuation of the species. Many, perhaps even most, human groups are still working under this theory. As an alternative to this objective perpetuation, other groups are operating with a subjective, religious goal and they may not give priority to secular perpetuation. The "reference group" I use is what I consider a typical group whose objective goal is to perpetuate itself in the natural world.

Different goals, or ends, require different means, or rules. Thus, ethical rules developed apply to only the specific group of people that has adopted a common primary goal. The rules are the means by which the group plans on accomplishing that goal. Taken as a whole, these rules can be called an ethical system. If a group has an ethical system with few rules, then the individuals within that group have maximum freedom to do as each pleases. A group with no rules has complete liberty. In such a group, differences in talent, ability, and other advantages will assure unequal accumulation of assets of the group. The group members will become unequal. At the other extreme, a group with many rules governs closely, restricting everything and everybody. Members of a group with many rules have minimum liberty. As a result, the more talented within the group are restricted, and there is much more equality among group members. The rules of all ethical systems must lie somewhere between minimal rules with maximum liberty but minimum equality, and maximal rules with maximum equality but minimum liberty. Ethics does not value one approach over the other. It only observes that, within any ethical system, more liberty results in less equality and more equality in less liberty. These values represent extremes along a continuum. If any group is to accomplish its goal, it must find an appropriate balance between these reciprocally related extremes. A corollary of this reciprocal relationship is that liberty permits competition and equality abhors competition. Competition, in fact, is the hallmark of liberty. Equality, on the other hand, does not permit competition since someone will come out the "winner" and the group will no longer be equal.

The process of developing, administering and applying the rules is politics. Note that politics is in no way inherently bad, but represents the vital process needed to develop and administer the group's ethics—the tangible product that results from balancing liberty and equality. Politics can be labeled "bad" (unethical) when the rules do not result in the maximum probability of survival and perpetuation of the group. Thus, it is bad (unethical) if the people involved subvert the process to their personal ends rather than the group's goal (end) of perpetuation. Note also that the process must always consider long-term as well as short-term consequences in considering the goal of perpetuation. Dealing only with the short-term consequences is another way politics can be bad (unethical). "In everything one must consider the end." With an objective goal, it is the definable testable end of perpetuation that counts.

The complete absence of rules results in "no holds barred" competition that, as elsewhere in nature, will eventually lead to the establishment of leadership by the most competitive. It is not likely that someone is so strong, egotistical and willful that they can assume control and ignore the rules of a reasonably functioning group. However, in times of anarchy, or in a group with few or weak rules, the "alpha dog" emerges and assumes leadership of the group. The situation of few rules permits the greatest individual liberty, the most competition and the greatest ego gratification. In some circumstances, it may be the best immediate solution available to the group. Philosophically, Nietzsche dubbed this "alpha dog" the *Übermensch,* usually translated as Superman. The appearance of a superman, or alpha dog, is the predictable result that will occur in a group with few or ineffective rules. Such groups are fragmented, inefficient and unable to restrain a particularly strong, talented or crafty individual. Nietzsche can be regarded as an avatar of Calicles, the character in Plato's *Republic* who decried that the weak make laws to hamper or get the better of the stronger. Each would advocate a system with few rules. Calicles and Nietzsche, then, can serve as our anchor for the liberty/competition end of the spectrum of ethical systems.

Buddha, Christ and Kant occupy the opposite end of the philosophic spectrum. Their systems maximize rules. The resulting restraints permit minimal competition and attempt to maximize equality. This is seen in Christ and Kant's maxim of "do unto others . . . " and Buddha's concept of an "egoless" system. These oppose the unrestrained ego permitted by complete liberty that results in the ascendancy of the alpha dog. This end of the spectrum favors maximum rules that equalize the strong and the weak. These systems are, thus, strongly against competition. Note the difference here between equality of value versus equality of opportunity among all members. The equality end of the spectrum assumes that members of the group are all of equal value and, hence, deserving of their "fair share" of the group's assets. The liberty end of the spectrum stresses equality of opportunity. This permits all to have equal access to competition within the group thereby selecting the most talented as leaders. The concept of equal opportunity is distinctly different from equality of value. Equality of value would divide the assets and satisfy needs equally among members regardless of the talent of the individual and regardless of his or her ability to be successful in competition. Unless otherwise specified, equality, in this book, is used to mean equality of value.

With an objective goal of perpetuation of the species, it is a given that some individuals will be more capable than others of helping the group to accomplish the goal. These members are of more value to the group. Only subjective goals can have the luxury of considering all members of the group as of equal value since this approach does not have an objective standard, or end, against which it is judged. As extreme examples, we can see that the terminally ill and the severely disabled are less useful and less important to the group than bright, healthy and talented 20-year-olds. It is, in fact, contingent on the group to identify the best and the brightest of their members and then use them according to their skills. Thusly, these more talented members can contribute maximally in helping the group to accomplish its primary goal. Some amount of liberty and competition are needed to find and use this talent. Specialization of the group in selecting the most talented farmers, soldiers, engineers or politicians, for example, requires competition among group members to allow the best to rise to assume their appropriate roles. As noted above, ensuring that all have access to the competition, equality of opportunity, is critical to make sure the group has identified its most talented members. Structuring the competition to best benefit the group is a fundamental role of ethics and the basis of equality of opportunity. Structuring the rewards commensurate with the value individuals bring to the group is also a fundamental role of ethics. The theory "from each according to their ability and to each according to their needs" has been well tested and falsified. These large group experiments in human history, including Russian communism, have shown equal distribution of assets will not consistently inspire the talented members of a group to work according to their abilities. Thus, in all larger groups, it can be taken as a given that some reward above the average is needed for more valuable members.

It is also seen as a given that, with the objective goal, other animals are not equal to human group members. The goal is to perpetuate the human species. Perpetuation of other animal species is important in the accomplishment of our human goal, but this does not ascribe equality to other animal species. I note that, in specific cases, some animals may be more important than some people. For example, a milk cow might be more useful to a group than a slightly demented, aged philosopher if the cow is important for survival of the humans and the philosopher expendable. Thus, the cow, in this situation, should be protected in preference to the philosopher. It is also not to say that cruelty to animals is appropriate. There are plenty of reasons why the group should avoid cruelty to animals—the primary one being the negative effect this would have on functioning within the human group. The reason is not, however, because other animals have equal rights. Equality of all animals, like equality of all group members, is a luxury that can be indulged in only with a subjective goal or with an objective goal that differs from perpetuation of the human species.

The liberty end of the spectrum, through competition, identifies the more talented group members and utilizes them to the advantage of the group. At the other end of the spectrum, involving equality, there is the need for numbers of members to form the backbone of the group. This will be the bulk of the members. Most members have some talent that will help the group. It is analogous to the structure of an army. The top general leads, but many lesser members are needed for the group to function properly. If done in ethical perfection, each member rises to his or her optimum station, according to ability and talent, with compensation proportionate to the talent and value they bring to the group. The young continue rising, and eventually the best of this generation will replace the former top general. Certainly, however, no one who has been in the army thinks it could be run without sergeants. Life outside of the army is no different. Many levels of talent are needed for the group to function best. Most group members are the privates, the captains and the sergeants, who labor at the many necessary jobs of the group, keep the infrastructure going and provide the foot soldiers for the generals. Those with limited talent also would help form the reservoir of the needed, diverse genetic pool for the next generation of the group.

The currently successful "leaders" of the group are ideally those most talented to face the current threats. However, the next threats to the group, at some future time, may well be entirely different and may well require entirely different talents and responses. It is important to sustain a certain number of members, with a diverse genetic pool, to handle the unknown of the future. It is then necessary to nurture and protect the developing youngest generation, the children, even before they can contribute to the group. Without enough spreading of the wealth and kindness to the youngest generation and the other less talented, the whole system will break down, if not in this generation then one in the near future. It is a resource problem for the group. With enough resources the group may be able to afford the luxury of maintaining even the least talented and least contributing members. Without sufficient resources, decisions must be made and some of the least talented with the least potential not sustained. Either end of the liberty-equality scale can be overbalanced. Within living memory the eugenics experiment of Nazi Germany took the strength side of the equation to extreme with unnecessary and unethical termination of those seen as less fit and less perfect. Still, the fact that such thinking can be abused cannot paralyze the group into overbalancing the scale toward equality. The toughest ethical decisions invariably involve deciding when it is appropriate for some of the less talented individual members to suffer in order for the group to have the best chance of surviving. This is a fundamental job of ethics and the objective goal will give a frame of reference as to how to make these tough decisions.

Once the goal of the group is defined, the successful ethical system governing the group adds or subtracts rules in order to accomplish the goal. The ethical system is successful if the goal is achieved. It is extremely unlikely that any group can give itself the maximum chance of long-term perpetuation operating from either extreme of liberty or equality. How many or how few rules the group chooses to enact represents a balancing of liberty and equality. It is in this balance that we find the necessary reconciliation of the strength of Nietzsche and the kindness of Christ. It is fundamental to understand that neither approach is inherently "right" or "wrong." Rules of any ethical system are judged by whether or not they accomplish the primary goal of giving the group its best chance of long-term survival.

Based on these concepts, I offer this description of an ethical system. An ethical system is the set of rules accepted by and applied to a specifically defined group of humans. These rules have the function of giving the group the best chance of accomplishing the primary goal of the group. While secondary goals may also be stated, priority will always be given to the primary goal. These rules, which necessarily balance the reciprocal values of liberty and equality, must be flexible over time to accommodate varying threats, available resources and changes in membership of the group. Changes in the ethical rules are resisted by the inertia of the traditions of the group. Politics is the development, application and administration of these rules for the group. Larger groups also have, within them, competition of subgroups and individual members trying to gain additional advantage for themselves. If done within the structure of the larger group's rules, this competition is ethical. It is an integral part of however much liberty is accepted by the group as necessary to identify its most talented elements.

The Holy Grail of an ethical/political system is to continually rebalance liberty and equality, adjusting to always give the group the maximum chance to accomplish its primary goal of perpetuation. A reasonable theory of group-coordinated function would predict that a smoothly functioning, coherent group working together would have the best chance of success. The problem is that all systems have strengths that, over time, become their weaknesses, and eventually force a change in the type of ethical/political system. The Platonic progression is well known from benevolent prince to tyrant to aristocracy to oligarchy to democracy to anarchy to alpha dog/*Übermensch*/prince. Then the pattern repeats itself. The free competition of anarchy may produce an unusually talented individual and perhaps a series of talented leaders. It is, however, a system that cannot last forever and eventually, as in the Roman Empire, Marcus Aurelius will pass the torch to a Commodus. To a very real extent, each type of political structure collapses because individuals and subgroups selfishly gratify their desires and ignore the needs of the larger group. This results in an imbalance of liberty and equality. Political/ethical systems must periodically change the rules to adjust to new circumstances. The dominating quality, whether liberty or equality, will give advantage to some members more than others. With liberty, the advantage is for the more talented. With equality, the advantage is for the less talented. For any given ethical political system, it is likely that this balance developed appropriate to the specific threats the group faced at a particular time. Those threats, however, always change. Those members with the initial advantage are unlikely to be willing to give up their advantage even if the threats are different and a change in balance is ethically required. By continuing to exploit that advantage, the balance then shifts even more in the wrong direction, hastening the demise of the current political form.

In the liberty extreme, the wealth and assets become more and more concentrated among fewer members. As in the proverbial "Banana Republics," this will predictably result in revolution of the increasing numbers of those with few assets. In the equality extreme, as in the fiction of Ayn Rand's *Atlas Shrugged* or some recent (in the last century) communist experiments, there ceases to be sufficient talent to run the group effectively. Neither system is changing to best counter the threats with which it is presented. They are changing, or not changing, to gratify the desires of individual members. In the liberty extreme, the few with most of the assets desire to keep it all, regardless of how it affects the group. In the equality extreme, the less talented want to be compensated as if they were talented, also regardless of how it affects the group. Both situations represent an unethical reversal of priorities. By advancing individual members' desires in front of the group's needs, they prevent the group from responding optimally to the threats it faces. This weakens the group and a weaker group is less competitive and less able to counter threats. This results in negative long-term ethical consequences for the group as it slides, seemingly inexorably, through the various political systems into the most vulnerable and weakened state of anarchy. Ethically, the system must change its balance of liberty and equality as necessary to act as an effective group so as to counter different threats. Members that block these changes to keep their personal advantages weaken the group. A weak group cannot give itself the best chance of perpetuation. By definition, this is unethical.

Philosophy does not say which of the above political systems is better. It must be realized that even democracy, while best for one group, may not be best for another group with different traditions and different education of its members. History shows, and philosophy can advise, that the extremes of liberty and equality have never worked for long and are not likely to do so in the future. The answer is in the balance. If either end of the Nietzsche–Christ scale gets too much advantage, then the system will most likely collapse. Broadly speaking, America breaks down identifiably into two camps (inconsistencies on both sides acknowledged) with the liberty end represented by the Republicans and the equality side represented by the Democrats. The lesson to be learned is that if either side "wins" the country will inevitably lose. Each group, Republicans or Democrats, has the temptation to work toward advantages for their subgroup, trying to keep their subgroup in power. Rather, they should be working to balance liberty and equality, which is what will do best for America. It requires recognizing that neither the Republican/liberty nor the Democratic/equality position alone can produce the ethical answers for America. Discussion, compromise and moderation are the necessary components of working out this balance. It is this ever-changing balance that produces ethical answers to the threats and problems the country faces and ensures long-term stability. The dark side of politics emerges when individuals or subgroups subvert equal opportunity competition to advance certain members when they are not the most talented, or when they seek advantage for their own subgroup, when that is not in the best interests of the larger group. It is also worth noting the obvious: if members of a group, e.g., young people in America, decide not to participate in the political system, then they will have no input into the ethics of the country. In addition, the country, working without them, may be using the less talented in needed political positions, a situation that in itself is unethical.

Ethics is the answer to the group's problem of survival. Ethical decisions are defined only as to their impact on the group in its efforts to achieve its primary goal. A perfect hermit, who lives with no significant impact on the environment on which we all depend, and never interacts with other humans, has no ethical problems. He can still have moral problems (see the section on Understanding the

Difference Between Ethics and Morals), but ethics represents the solution, the means, a group has decided on in order to solve the problem of perpetuation—the primary goal. No individual working alone can solve this problem. Hence, an individual working entirely alone is outside of all ethical considerations. Accordingly, throughout history, and no doubt in prehistory, man has organized himself into groups. The basic unit is the family and the largest unit is world humanity. In prehistory, groups started with immediate family, then extended family and tribe. Larger groups, which required better communication, developed more slowly. It is worth noting that, even in this earliest stage of group development when the rules were few and strength was of paramount importance, some rules requiring kindness, sharing and protection were needed within the group. Without such rules, it would have been unlikely that the weaker females and children could have survived and, thus, the group would have been unable to perpetuate itself.

Deontology deals with the duties and obligations of the group and its members. The functional definition of deontology is as follows: Deontology is the obligations and advantages agreed to between the group as a whole and its individual members that permits the formation, maintenance and efficient functioning of the group. If restricted to obligations, we miss half of the equation. There are definite advantages received by both parties, and it is for these advantages that members and groups assume the obligations. Advantages for one party are the obligations assumed by the other. Deontology is traditionally defined in terms of obligations and commitments, but each party—the members and the group—evaluates the value of the advantages it receives before it assumes the obligations. Using our objective frame of reference, and proceeding in the manner discussed in the section on data acquisition and processing, we will try to identify objective advantages and obligations that make group formation worthwhile

In summary, there is an objective quid pro quo that results from individuals joining or merging with a larger group. The new members get the advantage of protection, and the larger group gets the advantage of more members. The larger group assumes the obligation of protecting the new members. The members assume the obligation of following the rules of the larger group. Both parties use objective data to make sure that the partnership is good value. Note that even if a significant size subgroup decides to join a larger group, the deontological agreement is between the new, individual members and the larger group that is joined. It is not an agreement between the subgroup and the larger group. It is individual members who will have to follow the rules of the larger group and it is individual members who will have to be protected by the larger group. If the leaders of a subgroup agree to join a larger group but the members of the subgroup are not interested, then the new group formed will be unstable and inefficient since many of the new members will not follow rules that benefit the larger new group.

Individuals use the following data to decide if it is worthwhile to merge with the larger group. The larger group can provide the individuals much more protection, both from the vagaries of nature and from other groups of humans. Diversified larger groups can specialize, which allows them to better deal with more complicated threats and large-scale threats, including natural disasters or invasion. For example, a larger group can mitigate the disastrous effects from drought, earthquakes or tidal waves. Protection from invasion may be possible only if your group is large. This lack of protection, the negative side of not being a part of a functioning larger group, is expressed in Hobbes' famous comment from the *Leviathan,* " . . . and which is worst of all, continual fear and danger of violent death; and the life of man, solitary, poor, nasty, brutish, and short." The positive side of this concept is particularly well explained by Thomas Cahill in his discussion on the Roman Empire in his book *How the Irish Saved Civilization.* "The Britons, the Gauls, the Africans, the Slavs who long ago had flocked to the Roman standard, forsaking their petty tribal loyalties and becoming Roman citizens, gained greatly. By exchanging tribal identity for the penumbra of citizenship, they won the protection of the Pax Romana—and its predictability. With the decline of sudden unexpected violence of all kinds, they could look forward in a way they had never been able to before: they could plan, they could prosper, they could expect to live a normal life span."

If a group is to give itself the best chance of perpetuation, it must function unified and efficiently. Thus, in joining the larger group, the new members have to give up their "tribal loyalties" and prioritize the perpetuation of the new larger group. They do so with the prospect of having a better life with more personal happiness. It is, however, important to recognize that the members have not agreed to more than this. Thus, it becomes a corollary of the agreement that, while agreeing to follow the ethical rules of the larger group, the members may continue to pursue their own secondary goals—specifically religion and other forms of happiness. This is allowable as long as those pursuits do not compromise the achievement of the primary group goal. In fact, this is a major factor individuals consider prior to joining a larger group. They will analyze whether or not they will have a better chance of finding happiness as members of a larger group even though they would become ethically obligated to subordinate their personal goal of happiness to the larger group's goal of perpetuation. An objective theory of optimum group functioning would say that restricting individuals' pursuit of happiness, if such pursuit is not negatively affecting the larger group's primary goal, is itself detrimental to group functioning and hence unethical. This forms the unabridged version of the aphorism "The government is best that governs least." This is not to say that anarchy is the best form of government. What this statement says is that the rules of the group should be sufficient to ensure the common goal, but no more than that. Restrictions should not be placed on individual pursuit of happiness *unless* it is necessary to do this in order to protect the group's primary group goal.

The larger group benefits from increased membership up to the point its resources can support the larger numbers. Increased membership gives potential military strength. Increased numbers allow for specialization to counter different threats. Diversity from new members offers both new talent and more genetic possibilities that can expand the genetic pool, thus furnishing additional protection from possible illnesses and producing new talent. It can be less draining on the larger group to have the individuals of a smaller group join rather than to conquer or eliminate them.

If both parties see it to their advantage to merge, there are three requirements that must be met. They must both agree that they are members of the same species. That is, it cannot be seen as an up-down relationship. Joining members must be accorded equal opportunity to demonstrate their talent and thus help both themselves and the larger group. Note again that equal opportunity is not the same as equality. The larger group understands that the group needs the best talent working for it. The only way to know the best talent is being used is to make sure that all, including the new members, have the opportunity to show their worth. This requires equal opportunity to engage in the group-sanctioned competition.

The second requirement is the sine qua non—the keystone that supports the whole group structure. All members of the group must dedicate themselves to the primary goal of survival and perpetuation of the group. If joined, all members must follow the ethical rules of the group designed to give the group the best chance of perpetuation. The new individuals must take on the larger group's primary goal as their primary goal. Only with this one common goal can the group function optimally. Previous individual goals must become secondary. All members must "forsake their petty tribal loyalties" and place pursuit of happiness, including religion, in a secondary role. "Separation of Church and State" also means that the church is second. Nothing can be prioritized above the perpetuation of the group. The Venetians, much to the consternation of the Papacy, had it right. "We are Venetians first and Christians second."

The third requirement is that the rules, the ethics, of the group will be formed using objective data and theories so that all individuals can understand why the rules are what they are and that they are not formed capriciously or subjectively. Thus, new members, as well as old, can understand the data, logic and reasoning behind the rules they have agreed to follow. This objectivity requirement is generally accepted as key to theory formation, as is shown in Popper's work *The Logic of Scientific Discovery.* Philosophy's ethical theories are not exempt from this requirement and nor, for that matter, are they exempt from the falsifiable requirement.

A key feature of optimal group formation is that the requirements for membership are met and agreed to by both parties. Both parties have considered the pros and cons of joining and have decided that it is worth it. Both parties then accept the obligations that go along with the advantages of the merger. The larger group agrees to provide protection for the smaller group, *so long as the protection does not compromise the larger group's ability to achieve its primary goal.* All members of the group understand that, under severe stress, individuals may need to be sacrificed to save the larger group. This is like a military situation where a smaller unit must be left behind and sacrificed to protect the larger, retreating army. New members understand this one restriction but conclude that the protective advantages are still worth it. They agree to follow the rules and prioritization of the larger group and be effective ethical members of the group.

It is important to realize that if *either* party decides that the merger to form a common group is not worth it, then there are no obligations assumed between them. There is no quid pro quo. The smaller group is owed no protection and no kindness, and the larger group receives no talent or enlargement benefit. If the larger group then decides it is ethically necessary to acquire the resources of the smaller, nonmember group, they are restricted in their actions only by the long-term ethical consequences to their larger group. The long-term implication of how any group deals with outside groups is, however, a critical part of any ethical decision. Consider the example of treaties. Machiavelli advises that it is acceptable to not keep a treaty if so doing would be ruinous to your group. Under those circumstances, breaking a treaty can be entirely ethical. The group's first job is to ensure survival of itself, not to assist outside groups in their efforts to achieve different goals. The group is not restricted by the consequences breaking a treaty might have on an outside group. It is restricted, however, by the long-term consequences such actions might have on the group itself. The longer-term problems that arise from breaking treaties and other promises often mean it is in the group's best interest to honor treaties. The historical religious adage of not having to keep your word with infidels may occasionally apply, but *usually* it will be in your group's best interest to keep treaties.

As a member of a group, the individual is unethical if he or she acts in a manner that is detrimental to the group's goal of perpetuation. Unethical conduct may be unintentional (discussed below) but is more often motivated by self-interest. It occurs when members act to gratify their personal pursuit of happiness even though it will have a negative impact on the group. Remember the deontological agreement. The individual's part of the agreement was that he or she would prioritize the goal of the group The personal pursuit of happiness is thus a secondary goal. Although this requirement to act in the best interest of the group is more comprehensive than just following the written rules, the most obvious examples of unethical behavior occur when individuals break the laws (rules/ethics) of the group. It is assumed, for purposes of this topic, that the laws are based on the best objective data and theories and represent appropriate ethical behavior for the group. How to change inappropriate (unethical) laws is a separate question for ethics and involves politics.

The larger group as a whole can be unethical in three general ways: it can fail to provide protection to its members; it can interfere with an individual's pursuit of happiness when such pursuit is not detrimental to the ethical goal of the larger group; or it can restrict equal opportunity by not letting all members compete equally. Protection requires an active role on the part of the group as a whole. Failure to protect members is unethical, a "sin" of omission. Not interfering with members' pursuit of happiness requires a hands-off role by the group. Such inappropriate interference is unethical, a "sin" of commission. Failure to ensure equal opportunity has elements of each. It would be a sin of omission to deny individuals protection from unethical other members who would interfere with equal opportunity. It would also be a sin of commission to restrict equal opportunity since it intimately relates to an individual's pursuit of happiness. Even more important for the group, it is unethical because equal opportunity is vital in order to identify the best talent needed within the group.

Individuals have an understandable concern regarding the potential abuse of the power of the larger group towards individuals. Much of the American concept of government deals with how to protect the individual members from unneeded and unwanted governmental interference—how to assure that the governmental Leviathan will not act unethically. This is an important half of the problem. It is, however, only half, since not protecting the larger group from unethical individuals is equally detrimental and unethical. As noted above, there is an active role the government must ethically pursue to provide protection and ensure equal opportunity. The government can be unethical or individual group members can be unethical. The group has to be protected from both threats if it is to be ethical.

I use the word government to refer to the group as a whole, but it is important to recognize that the government is not a separate entity. Consider simpler groups such as tribes governed by tribal elders with widespread input from the other tribal members. As is clearly seen in this case, and also true for larger groups functioning ethically, government is not a separate entity. It is not the opposition. Government is the administrative process composed of some numbers of members of the group. Governing is the group's process for developing and applying the ethics of the group. The distrust of government occurs because those members of the group involved in governing may act unethically and use their position to selfishly benefit themselves or immediate friends to the detriment of the larger group. If they so act, they violate their ethical responsibility and may, in essence, form a different group that assumes a new top priority—that of perpetuating themselves in preference to the original group. If this happens, the members who make up the government may, in effect, become an opposing group. The power granted to those who govern makes this temptation great. Still, those members who govern must have power in order to make and enforce unpopular decisions that are ethical and needed by the group. The governing members are often placed in situations where data is incomplete and decisions are difficult. Invariably, some members particularly affected by these difficult decisions will think government has violated its trust and the governing members have selfishly succumbed to the temptation of power. Thus, the group must balance the power and latitude given its governing members. The group will try to have a governing system that restricts potential abuses but still permits appropriate difficult decisions to be made.

Describing unethical behavior by individual members or the group as a whole is another way of describing the obligations of each party in the agreement that resulted in the formation of the group. The obligations of one party constitute the advantages of the other party. Continuing to live up to these obligations is necessary if the group is to be maintained and progress optimally toward its goal. Failure to meet these obligations is by definition unethical. These mutual obligations make up a deontological contract. While it can be expressed as a series of obligations, it is important to realize that each obligation of one of the parties represents an advantage to the other party. Each party assumed the obligations only to gain the advantages.

Unethical actions regarding these obligations can be regarded as a broken contract even if the contract is not explicitly written down, a likely situation in smaller groups such as families. In larger, more complex groups, such as the United States, the obligations are formalized to eliminate subjectivity and ambiguity. The United States Constitution represents an excellent example of a written contract of a larger group forming from smaller component parts. The original members represented by the 13 original subgroups agreed to join to accomplish six specific ends stated in the preamble: " . . . in order to form a more perfect union, establish justice, insure domestic tranquility, provide for the common defense, promote the general welfare, and secure the blessings of liberty . . . " By logic and general agreement, common defense is prioritized since without this the others become irrelevant. All states, and by association the individual members of the states, through their representatives, swear to obey the ethical rules of the group by agreeing to obey the Constitution. The Constitution promises to protect the individual subgroups, the states (and again, by association, the individual members of the states). God is nowhere mentioned (except in the date at the end where A.D. is translated as the Year of Our Lord). The pursuit of happiness is not mentioned. However, the Constitution does guarantee all members that the government will not infringe upon the ability of individuals to pursue the specific happiness offered by religion. Equally important, that religion cannot be used as a determinant in selecting government officials. It is worth a passing comment that keeping any religious test out of the selection process of government officials was in the original Constitution and antedated by two years the first amendment that included keeping government out of the individual's religion as well as additionally specifying that government could not establish a religion. All subsequently joining members of this group, both new states and naturalized citizens, must swear an oath to uphold the Constitution. This is a good example of the mutual obligations of both parties in larger group formation presented in a formal contract.

The Declaration of Independence, on the other hand, is a document with an entirely different purpose. This document was composed to justify breaking a deontological contract that the colonies had with England. The grievances listed were the reasons why the colonies believed that England had not kept its side of the contract. This declaration detailed the basis for the colonies to break the contract. Although this dissolution was needed before the country could be formed, it is important to note that no new country was founded with the signing of this Declaration of Independence. The necessary war was yet to be won, but even then no new country, the United States of America, existed. That required a new deontological contract—the Constitution—to be created and signed. Until that happened, each colony considered itself a separate entity. It was no accident that in the Declaration of Independence the united States was written with a little 'u'. They were in agreement on getting out of the old arrangement, but they were not yet in agreement on creating a new country—a new group with mutual obligations and advantages. This came 11 years later. The Declaration of Independence did indulge in subjective persuasions that members could decide in their own minds what was meant. An objective listing of grievances justified breaking the old contract; however, the Declaration also included subjective self-evident truths and mention of a Creator. How self-evident, subjective "truths" were interpreted is interesting to ponder. Consider, for example, that the ringing phrase "all men are created equal" was written by Thomas Jefferson, a slave owner, and signed by many who were also slave owners. The terms "Creator" and "nature's God" were and are also subject to considerable variation in interpretation. Jefferson, for example, is claimed as a Unitarian. Even our most treasured, subjective phrase, "pursuit of happiness," appears only in the Declaration of Independence. The important deontological point here is that while subjective concepts were useful in dissolving the old contract, they were avoided in the new contract of the Constitution. It was the

Constitution that objectively specified the goals and obligations of the parties involved and formed the new country of the United States of America—with a capital 'U'.

There is an additional fundamental point to be understood in deontological contracts. That is that the contract is between the individual members of the group and the group as a whole, not between the various individual members within the group. An ethical contractual deontological theory would be more accurately titled *What We Each Owe the Group and What the Group Owes Each of Us,* rather than *What We Owe Each Other,* the title of a book by T.M. Scanlon. Ethically, he or she is required by the terms of the contract to treat other members of the group appropriately because of the effect such treatment has on the group—not primarily because of the effect on another individual. Even egregious individual assaults such as rape and murder are, ethically speaking, an assault on the group and a violation of the deontological contract with the group. (It is true that these acts are usually also considered immoral individual assaults, but morals differ from ethics and we will discuss these differences in a later section.) The theory behind the deontological contract says that the terms are designed to first assure the group can perpetuate itself. Failure to treat other members properly results in a fragmented, inefficient group that does not have the best chance of perpetuation. It is unethical because of its effect on the group. Individual members receive advantages and have assumed the obligations of the contract to ensure the group survives. Individual members make secondary contracts between themselves and other members. Ethically they are required to keep these contracts, which include the virtues and do-unto-others, because they must do so to fulfill their obligations to the group to help the group function most efficiently in the accomplishment of the group's primary goal. Clearly defining the parties involved in the primary, group-member deontological contract helps us gain insight as to why secondary contracts, such as promises between individual members of the group, can be preempted by the prioritized terms of the primary contract between the individual and the group. We keep promises because it is good for the group. Ethically, we can break a promise if it is better for the group that it is broken.

An objective goal means that there are no loopholes, no excuses for unethical behavior. If what is done harms the ability of the group to accomplish its primary goal then it is de facto unethical. Ethics does not confine itself to the written rules the politics of the group produces. Likewise, just because the rules are written down, they are not necessarily ethical. All individual and group actions are eventually judged by whether or not they worked. Members have the obligation to do the best they can to make sure that the group can accomplish its primary goal. If actions prove disadvantageous to the group, they are unethical, even if they were well intended. This could be said to be a variation on the aphorism "the road to hell is paved with good intentions." The final judgment of ethical or unethical is retrospective based on results. Ongoing review of the rules based on the group's ethical theories is important in order to see what worked and what did not. This ongoing review is the practical application of the testability requirement of objective theories. Retrospective judgment is needed for what the business world calls quality improvement. You do not want to make the same mistakes again no matter how good the intentions. The group has a theory that such and such is ethical. The theory is falsified because it doesn't work. Now the group needs a better theory.

Another implication of the objective goal is that there are no degrees of "good." We can equate ethical with good and unethical with being bad. The expression "for the good of the group," or "the greatest good," is used in this book to mean "that which gives the group the best chance of perpetuation." If you are in compliance with the rules, the ethics, of the group, you are in compliance. It is like being perfect. You cannot be more perfect. Every job is important. Doing your job as well as you can and always treating other members appropriately puts you in compliance. There are, however, degrees of being unethical. Throwing a cigarette butt out the window is unethical, but it is not as bad as shooting 20 people at a restaurant. Our concept of the imprecise term evil is that it is maximally unethical. If you rank unethical behavior from 1 to 100 then "evil" could be said to cover those actions in the 90s. Some jobs are more important to the group than others, but everyone doing a job right is equally ethical. Doing a job wrong, however, can be less or more unethical. A brilliant military general is more valuable to the group than a nurse that takes care of the wounded. Still he or she is not more ethical if he or she does the job well. Conversely, a general can be more unethical if he or she performs poorly or inappropriately. Poor job performance on the part of the general can result in the group not surviving. Poor job performance on the part of the nurse loses only a few lives. The leader's role puts him or her in the position of being able to be more unethical. Quisling's actions for Norway and Joseph McCarthy's actions in the U.S. political arena demonstrate unethical actions with far-reaching negative consequences. The effects each had on their country were worse, more unethical, because of their leadership positions.

It is for the advantages of being a member of a larger group that the members of smaller groups combine and assume the resultant obligations. It started in prehistory with the family and extended family or tribe and group size has increased since then. Throughout time, the basic subgroup unit has been the family, and birth associations continue to be a strong contributing factor in determining who gets admitted into what group. Our word "nation" reflects this fact, as it derives from the Latin word meaning "to be born." At some evolutionary point, man developed the blessing (or curse) of awareness. With this, or perhaps in addition, man developed an increasing ability to communicate. It is improved communication that has enabled larger more efficient groups to form. Ian Tattersall theorizes, in the January 2000 issue of *Scientific American*, that it was the developed talent of communication that gave Homo sapiens the competitive edge over the Neanderthals in Europe. The Neanderthals had a thriving culture in Europe for perhaps 100,000 years, but humans, who arrived later, appear to have done away with all of them in the relatively brief period of 10,000 to 25,000 years. The point is this: the ability to communicate, and thus work effectively within larger groups, provides a significant advantage for survival and perpetuation.

Human groups continued to expand in size and complexity. Competition, operating according to the Darwin/Spencer (Darwin's ideas, Spencer's phrase) theory of survival-of-the-fittest, predominated. The competition was not only against the Neanderthals, but also against nature and against other human groups—man against man. The survival-of-the-fittest is a fact of nature and, as we have discussed, it is an effective means of perpetuating the species. It accepts lethal competition as useful for weeding out the less fit. Man, and many life forms that are still here, are proof of the success of the application of this theory. Eliminating or subjugating a less fit group was and is ethically acceptable under this theory. Understanding this competitive theory gives insight as to why one group with ethical rules of protection for its own members does not necessarily extend those rules to protect members of another group. A group's ethical rules cover only that group's members. They are not necessarily extended to outsiders who have a different goal and may, in fact, be trying to eliminate the group. Thus, the virtually ubiquitous "do-unto-others" principle applies only within a group.

Competition for survival has stimulated the formation of larger groups since these are less likely to be eliminated than smaller groups. Only recently, within the last century, has communication improved to the point where man can now consider forming a single world group. Because of changing threats and worldwide problems, I propose that man can best stave off extinction by becoming a single world group. I believe it is time to transition out of the lethal competition permitted by the traditional survival-of-the-fittest ethical theory. Like all group formation agreements, forming a single world group will require a deontological contract and, thus, it is contingent upon the advantages for each joining member outweighing the obligations that must be assumed.

For the moment let us assume that the population of the world is operating as a single group with all countries and other subgroups adopting the primary goal of perpetuation of the human species. If functioning optimally, each subgroup will prioritize in an upward fashion. The individual will put the good of the family first, the family will put the good of the town first, the town will put the good of the state first, the state will put the good of the country first, and the country will put the good of the world first. No subgroup is as important as the country, and even the country is not as important as the world. This large group unit is a fractal-like structure, built from repeating units with the fractal quality of self-similarity. At each level the functional structure has the same appearance in advantages and obligations, from the basic family unit up to the world of humanity as a whole. Only the world group has no higher obligation.

It might seem obvious why weaker members would join the world group. Protection, mitigation of disasters and more kindness and help than they could expect if they stayed out of the group constitute clear advantages for them. From the inside of the world group, protection means they are ethically not subject to the exploitation that might still be acceptable were they to stay on the outside as competitors. But why would strong, talented members want to join the world group and assume restrictive obligations? Remember that deontology is a structure that functions because it has advantages as well as obligations. The obligations are assumed only because it is worth it. For it to work, the advantages, even for the most talented and strongest, must always outweigh the obligations. Currently, the strongest member of the world group is the United States. Yet even the United States has threats that are worldwide in scope and cannot be effectively dealt with from one corner of the globe. Examples of such threats include the exploding world population, degradation of the environment, diminishing ocean resources, worldwide diseases, asteroids hitting the earth, an interdependent worldwide economy, and dangerous rogue subgroups with goals antithetical to perpetuation. Also, the technology of war has outstripped the ability of the world to withstand an all-out war. Historically, war has been the final competition involved in survival-of-the-fittest. Our current existence can be seen as the success of this approach in weeding out the less fit. Today, technology, particularly nuclear weapons but chemical and biological weapons as well, means that this form of all-out competition could immediately eliminate humans. It is no longer consistent with the goal of perpetuation. By definition, it is unethical for any group to not give itself the best chance of accomplishing its primary goal—perpetuation. War can no longer effectively manage all of the worldwide threats—particularly the environmental and over-population threats—mentioned above. Without worldwide cooperation, war cannot even manage the rogue subgroups. In addition, the interdependent economies, including the

United States, would be devastated by the all-out competition of war. It is then advantageous for even the strongest group to join the world group because it is the best way to be able to respond to these and other threats that are worldwide in scope and can affect the ability of even the strongest to perpetuate. They do assume obligations to the world group. These obligations will limit their freedom and liberty to act without considering how such action will affect the rest of the world. These restrictions are assumed only because the advantages received make it more likely that they can have the best chance of perpetuation.

To act ethically, the strongest, most talented member of any group, including the strongest country in the world group, must review history and accept that the top spot is a rotating position, one that changes with time and different circumstances. Times change, threats change, work habits change, resources change and, voila, the circumstances that enabled one country to be the "best" disappear. The factors that enabled one country to be the most competitive at any given time always change. The result is that the strongest most talented member again becomes one of the pack and another member, more competitive in the new environment, rises to assume leadership. That's the way the liberty/competition aspect of ethics works. You need the most talented at the moment leading the way, but it is foolish indeed to think that member will always be the same. His time in that position will be limited. It's part of the old business adage "Be nice to people on your way up the ladder because you'll meet them again on your way back down." The arrogance of the alpha dog, whether a country or an individual, is a problem for ethics and philosophy. This arrogance is behind the aphorism "Absolute power corrupts absolutely." In the case of a country in the dominant position, it will likely be a future generation that will climb back down the ladder. For this reason, it is difficult for the current generation to account for inevitable decline in its ethical planning. This difficulty is an ethical failure regarding long-term planning. More attention to long-term planning, making some short-term sacrifices, would be the ethical approach and would, in all probability, delay the decline. Ethics requires forward thinking, and the current alpha dog cannot make narrow decisions that will jeopardize the ability of future generations to survive.

The keystone to all group formation is that each member must prioritize the group's primary goal. Joining a single world group means that the priority shifts from each country perpetuating only itself to the priority of perpetuating world humanity—the species Homo sapiens in general. It is a shift from the theory of survival-of-the-fittest as the best way to perpetuate the species, to the world acting as a single group as the best way to perpetuate the species. If the threats are such that advantages outweigh obligations, I see no reason why even the strongest, secular countries would not join. Today, however, smaller groups are more likely to resist joining the larger world group or, for that matter, to be unwilling to join country-size groups. Jingoism, ethnic and tribal loyalties and religion cause subgroups to be unwilling to become members of a world organization. Such groups may not be willing to place the good of the larger group in front of the goal of perpetuation of their ethnic subgroup or in front of the subjective goal of sustaining the subgroup's particular religion. If the nonjoining groups are unwilling to assume the obligations within the larger world group, then these smaller groups will have to be dealt with. If they are unwilling to assume the obligations they are not entitled to the benefit of protection. Perhaps they can be ignored if they do not negatively affect the world group. If, however, they are negatively affecting the world group then the response from the larger group will need to be in a manner that is most consistent with the larger world group's ethical goal. The world group can fashion a response ranging from obliteration of the smaller group to withdrawal of privileges and resources. While it seems likely that, between hand slapping and obliteration, the least severe but still effective punishment would be best, it needs to be remembered that if elimination of the subgroup is best for the larger group then, ethically speaking, the subgroup needs to be eliminated. By not assuming the obligations, the smaller group is not entitled to any advantage of protection from the larger group. The larger group is under an obligation to the members of the group to respond in the manner that makes long-term accomplishment of the larger group's goal of perpetuation most likely. While, I hope, the survival-of-the-fittest theory is being phased out and we are moving toward a single world group approach to perpetuation, it is the potential necessity of having to manage the outlying groups with violent means that requires a military be well maintained. If violent means are required to ensure the goal, then it is unethical not to use such response.

It is my opinion that humans and human predecessors, wittingly or unwittingly, have always operated with this primary objective goal of group survival and perpetuation. So far we have been successful. There is, however, another selection that is and has been influential. This selection does not use an objective goal but bases the rules of the group, their ethics, on the subjective goal of perpetuating a particular religion. The problem, as with all subjective goals, is that there can be no sustained general agreement among humans as a whole group on either the basis or the result of the goal. Religion is a very important source of happiness for individuals and as such will be considered in the next section on esthetics and metaphysics. What is important to note here is that, because of its subjective nature and lack of a common frame of reference, religion is an unpredictable wild card in establishing ethical systems.

Functionally speaking, theocracies are not regarded as another form of political structure like democracy or aristocracy. What separates theocracies is that they have a subjective goal of perpetuating their particular religion rather than the objective secular goal of perpetuating the group/species. Regardless of what political form they take (dictatorship, oligarchy, etc.), theocracies are subject to the same frailties as objective, secular, goal-based political/governmental structures. They will, however, make their rules, ethics, based on the subjective ideals of the religion and not necessarily on secular reality or necessity. By using an alternative primary goal, one that is subjective, these groups can come into conflict both with other groups using different subjective religious goals as well as with secular groups based on the objective goal of perpetuation. The divergent subjective goals of theocracies make it difficult, if not impossible, for them to fully join the world's secular groups. The conflict is predictable since this subjective, religious approach violates the basic point made in the section on epistemology and logic: the only way all or most members of the larger group (in this case the world group of humans) can come into agreement is by using objective data and theories. The lack of an objective goal means that within theocracies (and also true of smaller religious groups) everybody can use their own subjective opinions to determine ethical acts. Individual factions can vary widely—from benevolence to violence. There is no common frame of reference. All of the multiple sacred texts used by various religions are subject to widely differing interpretations even within a particular religion and, needless to mention, there is almost no agreement that another religion's text is acceptable. A religion's ethics need accomplish only what each individual believes. This can permit, for some, obliteration of the human species, as these individuals operate under a theory of "kill them (us) all and let God decide." This is not a difficult rationalization if one subjectively believes that the most important goal is achieved only after death.

It is important to acknowledge that religion can make many positive contributions to the ethics of the group. Later, I will deal with the differences between individual morals, including those derived from religion, and group ethics. Suffice it to say at this juncture that there is usually considerable overlap between the ethics of the group and the morals of the group's religions. Often one reinforces the other. Religion can be helpful, some would say indispensable, in filling a role as the group's "supernatural policeman." Religion's morals invariably include some form of "do unto others," a well-tested theory necessary for group formation, coherence and efficiency. Morals, as defined by a religion, have often formed the starting point, the cornerstone, of a group's ethics. While this religious moral base can be a sea anchor in troubled times, it can be an inappropriate anchor as times change and different approaches are needed

There are consequences for groups that put religious rules in front of the objective good of the group. First, as small groups within a larger group, they can accept the advantages of protection without assuming all of the obligations of being a group member. This is unethical. These individuals and subgroups can form an unethical element within the larger group by refusing to follow the secular group's rules in preference to their subjective religious rules. Examples include religious pacifism that restricts military participation, and the refusal to use birth control when it is needed to restrict population. Second, larger-sized religious-based countries can be outliers from the secular world's primary goal of perpetuation in the natural world. Some of the religious may see the secular world as threatening to the religious goal they have assumed. As with any group, members will do whatever they think necessary to protect their primary goal. If that includes all-out war, even nuclear or biologic war, these religious elements can justify such action. Since all such thoughts are subjective, they cannot be gainsaid. It is ironic, that religion, to which most of us look for peace and tranquility, has been and continues to be a significant cause of wars and a major threat, perhaps the major threat, to the objective goal of long-term survival of the species.

Ethical rules can be divided into two types: the primary rules that deal with direct physical and environmental problems such as invasion, environmental degradation and diminished resources; the secondary rules that deal with group formation and effective group functioning. Both are based on objective data.

Primary rules deal with tangible, objective threats or problems. Since the threats change, the rules must change to appropriately counter the different problems. For example, too many people for available resources requires population control. Conversely, too few people for defense or various jobs requires increased population and encouragement of a high birth rate. Primary rules change over time with different situations. Still, if the process is done correctly, they are "infallible" for the moment. Since primary rules are dealing with specific, tangible threats to the group as a whole, they always take precedence over secondary rules. On occasion there may need to be prioritization even among the primary rules. Imminent threat of obliteration of the group, for example, takes precedence over longer-term considerations. It is a necessary part of ethics that the least unethical action may be the best that can be done and, thus, prioritization among ethical rules may be required in order to do what is best for the group.

The secondary ethical rules, involving group formation and efficiency, are based on the obligations in the deontological contract. The secondary ethical rules, regarding the obligations of the members to the larger group, are centered on the concept of "do unto others." These are the virtues, such as civility, honesty and courage, proved through the centuries to be necessary for efficient group functioning. The theory supporting the group use of "do unto others" has been well tested throughout history. The other set of secondary rules are the obligations the larger group has to the individual members. These are centered on the obligations of protection and equal opportunity. Failure to keep the obligations of the deontological contract—these secondary ethical rules needed for internal group maintenance—results in an inefficient, weak group. Weak groups cannot deal as effectively with threats and, sooner or later, are eliminated.

Secondary rules can, however, be overruled and they can be suspended as needed to accomplish the primary ethical rules of the group. The primary rules represent objective solutions required to handle the short-term exigencies and long-term threats directly related to survival and perpetuation. They must take precedence over the secondary rules that are important, but secondarily so, involving group cohesion and efficient functioning. Thus, breaking a promise to a fellow member can be ethical if it would be for the good of the group. Likewise, the group may be making the best ethical choice in choosing to not protect some of its weaker members if resources become limited. The group must always give itself the best chance of survival and perpetuation. The basis for the secondary position of the deontological obligations, the secondary rules, is simple. If the group does not physically survive, secondary rules become irrelevant. Of course, inappropriate violation of the secondary rules is unethical. If violation of the secondary rules is prolonged, and without cause based on the primary rules, it results in weakening and eventual dissolution of the group. The primary rules must change over time to face different threats, while the secondary rules remain remarkably stable since the rules needed for dependable interpersonal relationships required for group formation and maintenance change very little. Still, if there is a variance between primary and secondary rules, the group's changing primary needs will always overrule the secondary rules.

We will note that if a person is not in the group, if a person has not assumed the obligations required to join the group, then they are not entitled to the advantages of group members. They are not entitled to the advantages of "do-unto-others," and they are not entitled to protection by the group. This bothers us. We know they are people like us. It is quite uncomfortable to realize those outside our group are not entitled to be treated the same as our fellow group members. Treating all humans the same, however, awaits the formation of one-world group. Then, all concerned would assume the obligations that go along with receiving these advantages and we could stop, or at least limit, expending resources fighting each other in survival-of-the-fittest. Then, humans could much better address the problems we all have in common and best develop the primary ethical rules we all must follow to counter these threats. At that point, all would be entitled to be treated equally regarding the secondary rules since all would be members of the same group trying to perpetuate the species. We must remember, however, that point is not yet here. Practically and ethically speaking, at this time in history, the secondary ethical rules still do not apply equally to all.

Reason and awareness, while not qualifying as our most important functions, are cited as special functions of human beings. They may or may not be unique in the animal kingdom but, regardless, these special functions impose on us the requirement that we consider long-term implications of our conduct. This is particularly important in determining appropriate primary ethical rules. We can reason that we, the current generation, each and every one of us, will die. If we follow our prime directive of giving human beings the best chance of perpetuating the species, then we absolutely must act in this generation appropriately—ethically—to enable future generations to continue working towards this goal. We cannot think just in terms of our current generation and short-term quick fixes. We must see our position as a link in the chain, acknowledging our debt to our earlier generations who enabled us to be here, then acting so that future generations can continue the species. It is a critical part of ethics since only by so doing can we fulfill our goal.

It may be helpful to think of any ethical system as part of a process that is composed of three sets of variables. The first set of variables involves threats and changes imposed on the group. These include the amount of available resources, environmental challenges and changes in composition of the group. Also threats might include invasion and aggression by neighboring groups, population changes in your group and neighboring groups and so on. These are changes that always occur over time and to which any system must respond. More broadly speaking, time is no more than the measure of the rate of change of the universe. Changes are inevitable, and many changes are not under the control of the group. Still, some of the threats and stresses of any current generation could most likely have been avoided by better conduct of the forefathers. For example, environmental issues such as over-fishing cod, eliminating the passenger pigeon, and pollution of land and water all might have been avoided by appropriate actions of a previous generation. However, the current generation has no control over these factors.

The second set of variables is conduct—how the group decides to respond to the changing threats and circumstances. Does recommended conduct remain unchanged or do the new threats require different recommendations? This conduct provides the means for the group to counter life's changes. These rules, these means of reacting, are ethics. The group controls this set of variables.

The third set of variables is the "ends." We can set up an ethical system with an objective goal or a subjective goal or we can set up a system based on having a desired means that becomes the goal. This last system assigns top priority to behaving in a certain manner. It may choose to focus, like Kant, on the secondary rules of the deontological contract (as noted previously, usually based on some variation of do-unto-others). Or these systems may focus on past traditions or religious rules, which are considered too important to change. The consequences of this conduct, the ends, assume a secondary role. Regardless of the threats, these systems choose to let their means, their conduct, remain unchanged. This is de facto a means-determines-the-ends approach. Regardless of which basis is used, something will result, and it is inescapable (even if the system is labeled deontological) that there will be a consequence, from acting in the prescribed manner. These consequences, or "ends," will be the final product of the theory on which the ethical system is based. A group, following the rules of its ethical system, will have some end. The only question is how much control the group decides to use in order to influence the end. That, in turn, depends on how much importance the group decides to assign to the end. Systems that are unwilling or unable to effectively change their ethics—their means—when challenged by different threats may well lose control of their ends. Their means has become their ends. These groups may have to (perhaps must be willing to) accept elimination in order to leave their means unchanged. A group is much less likely to be able to perpetuate itself without an ethical system that places perpetuation as its most important end. For these groups, the end of perpetuation does indeed justify changing the means when necessary.

The common approach to developing ethical theories is to use inductive reasoning. This type of approach starts with the second variable—the means—and bases ethics on the identification of what is considered desirable conduct. Hume's approach is, perhaps, the prototype as stated in *An Enquiry Concerning the Principles of Morals:* by using "personal merit" and identifying "estimable qualities on the one hand, and the blamable on the other; and thence to reach the foundation of ethics . . . " Hume and his followers acknowledged this as inductive reasoning, but their acknowledgement in no way makes it more acceptable. Trying to argue from the particular to the general is well known to be suboptimal and represents fallible reasoning. Popper noted this specifically in his quote from *The Logic of Scientific Discovery,* " . . . any conclusion drawn in this way may always turn out to be false."

Collecting data in an inductive fashion can certainly be useful and has proved so in science. This collection is the objective data. The next step is to develop a deductive theory to accommodate the data. In philosophy, we can collect the behavior traits considered desirable (such as the virtues). The data would say that these traits are *usually* ethical. Exceptions would, however, be noted, and unless we can accommodate the exceptions with a deductive theory, we are left saying that such and such a virtue has a certain percentage chance of being ethical. For example, as pointed out earlier, there are exceptions to the rule of keeping promises. Writers from Machiavelli in *The Prince* to Foot in *Natural Goodness* have noted some of these. One could say that, generally, within one's own group, keeping a promise is very likely to be ethical and not keeping a promise is very likely to be unethical. Keeping promises with members outside of one's own group would still most likely be ethical, but the probability is less than with fellow group members. This approach means that the standard deviation of this probability varies. Nonetheless, theory formation can deal with probabilities. It could be calculated that keeping promises has, perhaps, a 98.3 percent chance of being ethical within one's group and, perhaps, a 95.6 percent chance of being ethical dealing with outsiders.

Take as an example this situation of a broken promise. The little Dutch boy promised his mother he would return home promptly by 6 o'clock for the family reunion honoring his grandparents' 50th wedding anniversary. He left in plenty of time to get home, but on the way he noticed a hole in the dike. He stopped to put his finger in the hole and thereby saved the town. He had to break his promise to do this and he missed the family reunion. Inductively basing an ethical structure wholly on "estimable qualities," in this case the keeping of promises, does not allow us to accept that his breaking the promise was ethical. At best, it could be said that his breaking the promise was part of the 1.7 percent when, statistically, it is ethical to do so. I contend that a probability spread describing exceptions, inherent in all inductive approaches, indicates that we need a better theory.

In *A History of Western Philosophy,* Bertrand Russell states, "One of the defects of all philosophers since Plato is that their inquiries into ethics proceed on the assumption that they already know the conclusions to be reached." It does not have to be that way. This book describes a theory that is based on an objective frame of reference. I contend that using perpetuation of the species as a common goal furnishes us with the "first premise" needed for a deductive approach. *We are to conduct ourselves in a manner that maximizes the chances of perpetuating the human species.* We can and will vary the means in order to achieve our goal. Most of the time we will keep our promises and we will follow "do-unto-others." However, if detrimental to the goal—our "greatest good"—we do not follow these precepts. It is important that we do not mistake the means for the goal.

It is also important we do not substitute individual goals and desires for the group's common goal. Later, I will discuss the other leading contender for a deductive approach—happiness. Individual happiness versus the group's goal of perpetuation will prove to be the biggest area of conflict in philosophy. The acceptance of the primacy of the goal of perpetuation forces us to realize that the essence of ethics lies in recognizing that there are occasions when one must recommend conduct that is not good for the individual or a smaller group. The writers Koch and Epstein summed this up at the end of *Casablanca*. Rick (Bogart) is speaking to Ilsa (Bergman) as they are forgoing their personal happiness and parting in order to help the allied cause. "But I've got a job to do . . . it doesn't take much to see that the problems of three little people don't amount to a hill of beans in this crazy world." Correct ethical priorities are maintained. The job is more important than their personal happiness. We acknowledge a more important goal. We will act so the group does not die, even if we have to sacrifice our personal happiness, or even life, to prevent the group's death.

While we do not have to be egoless to be ethical, we cannot be selfish if it hurts the group. "Ethical egoism" is an oxymoron. I consider the Prisoner's Dilemma*, which poses primarily an individual's problem, not to be a good ethical problem. There is considerable overlap between what is good for individuals and what is good for the group but, inherently, the individual ego's outlook is short term—a single life span. The group outlook must be both short term and long term—multiple generations. The difficult decisions occur when ethics begins to describe when it is unethical to be egotistical.

Investigation of egoism, no doubt, has a role in making recommendations for smooth group functioning, which is, as noted in the secondary ethical rules earlier, an important component in

---

*The Prisoner's Dilemma assumes that there are two prisoners and the punishment of each prisoner, regardless of guilt, depends on whether the other prisoner pleads guilty or not. The object in considering the options offered assumes that the only goal is to protect one's own interests and, thus, I do not consider this popular philosophical problem a good ethical problem but, rather, a problem for individual happiness.

the process of developing ethical decisions and conduct. Ethics says that there are interests that are more to be considered and more important than the individual. Spinoza was not correct in assuming that self-preservation is the foundation of virtue leading to ethics. Rather, preservation of the human species as a group is the foundation leading to ethics. When you accept this assumption, then, even though there is often overlap between what is good for the individual and what is good for the group, there is no basis for egoism forming ethical theories. There is always a priority of interests governing our ethical actions. The individual is last in line—behind family, behind town, behind state, behind country, behind the world.

Some would say the goal is in a supernatural world. They would say God has already specified ethics and to make any change in these ethical rules jeopardizes their afterlife. The end these individuals see is not objective. I have discussed that this approach, at best, cannot result in a unified vision for the group of humans as a whole. At worst, it results in fragmentation of humanity into different faiths that may result in lethal competition trying to prove the unprovable—that their religion is the best. It may lead to a faith-based continuation of survival-of-the-fittest. The technology, particularly nuclear weapons now available, speaks for itself in terms of potential disastrous effects such competition could have on the earth and its occupants. The loss of humanity from the natural world is too big a risk to allow dependence on people's widely varying, subjective belief systems regarding the supernatural. The one most important objective end, perpetuation of the species, overrides all other considerations.

All means, all conduct, must be available to the group with one categorical exception. No means can be used that will, in and of itself, eliminate humans from existence. War, in its place, can be ethical, and tactical nuclear weapons can be ethical. However, the concept of Mutually Assured Destruction, MAD, is ipso facto unethical. Over the next few decades (centuries or millennia may be a better time frame) it is overwhelmingly likely that war will continue to be a necessity of group perpetuation. Even with a much more unified world humanity group, military strength and some form of war will still be needed to deal with outlying subgroups.

Even in recognizing this fact, however, we cannot condone extremes in warfare or other environmental destruction that jeopardize the human race.

In spite of periodic, necessary changes to some of the rules/ethics of the group, most elements will remain the same. These represent recommendations based on well-tested theories that will not be changed unless some new theory proves clearly better. Groups try hard not to "throw out the baby with the bath water." These rules/ethics that are proved to work are retained and become the traditions of the group. These traditions provide stability for the group. However, as threats and resources change, successful groups will change the rules/ethics, even the traditions, to accommodate these different threats. We live in a natural world with a verifiable goal. We like to think that our ethics are written in stone. In fact, this is a perfect analogy. We can think of our forefathers as having chiseled their ethical system in stone. Yet, when we walk through the cemetery of our forefathers and view their headstones, we see what happens to that which was written even in stone. Like the older graveyard headstones, in a few generations time, different threats and altered resources will have radically changed their ethical stone slate. Palimpsest like, we now chisel in the same stone our current ethical system, saving what we can, but changing what we must. Future generations will then rechisel over what we have done. This is how it should be, building on the past but changing for the future. The most unethical thing would be to fail to perpetuate our human species.

ESTHETICS AND METAPHYSICS

WHY IS MAN WILLING TO DO THIS JOB?

"That life is worth living is the most necessary of all assumptions, and were it not assumed, the most impossible of conclusions."
—George Santayana, *Reason in Common Sense*

We now have our goal and job description, and we understand that ethics provides us with the rules to accomplish this job. We also realize that these rules, ethics, must be periodically adjusted in order to get the job done. The obvious next question is, "What's in it for me?" The answer to that question is addressed in the category of philosophy comprised of esthetics and metaphysics. The answer will be subjective, nonmeasurable to others and individualized. Thus, each of us will be rewarded differently. The generic value most often assigned to this answer is happiness. That is to say, the reason we are willing to do the job is because we derive happiness. Many other words could also be used to express the payback for doing this job, including contentment, pleasure, satisfaction or more encompassing concepts of self-fulfillment or self-actualization. Each of our individual "life trips" is relatively brief but, still, it is important that we each enjoy the trip. Each individual subjectively determines the quantity or value of the reward. It is not determined by objective standards. It is here that our subjective theories can shine so long as they do not negatively impact on the group's goal. It is this concept, for which philosophy uses the term happiness, that makes a life that is, in Santayana's words, "worth living." Functionally, esthetics is not defined by what it *is* but rather by what it *does*. Thus, the functional definition of esthetics is "that which gives an individual happiness."

This functional definition obviously differs from the traditional definition of esthetics—the study of ideal beauty. This discussion of philosophy is based on organization and function, philosophy as a coherent whole that regards each area by what it does. The ultimate product of philosophy is the ever-changing code of ethics needed to accomplish our primary goal. Each area of philosophy can be defined as ethical or unethical by what it accomplishes in contributing to species survival. In this section the philosophy of art is considered. From a functional point of view, the purpose of art is to be pleasing, to give happiness. Happiness is the necessary "pay check" we receive in our lives. It is the payoff for what many have regarded as a brief role, a "brief candle." The role, however, does not "signify nothing." It is important, much more than "sound and fury," if we want human existence to be a long-running production. Happiness is critical, for it must be commensurate with the importance of our part in the continuum. Ideally, we should be neither underpaid nor overpaid but, always, some will seek an inappropriate, excess allotment of happiness pursuing selfish, unethical behavior. With an objective goal, the role of philosophy is to brand such activity unethical and deal with it according to the group's rules. In fact, the biggest stumbling block in the path of perpetuation is in defining and dealing with people who act in their own self-interest, pursuing their own happiness, when such actions are detrimental to the group's success—the greatest good.

Art and beauty are the sources of esthetic happiness and pleasure, but the terms need to be thought of more broadly than we usually do. Each of us is an artist in our own right in experiencing the satisfaction of a job well done. Quantitatively, the appreciation of things deemed esthetic (beautiful or artistic) must give an individual sufficient happiness so that he or she is willing to do his or her primary job—perpetuate the species. What is esthetic, what produces happiness, is each person's individual subjective value judgment and is entirely personal. Indeed, beauty and happiness are measured in the "eye of the beholder." Thus, each person's artistic esthetic reward is varied and cannot, and need not, be quantifiable, other than to be sufficient for the individual. This reward of happiness is derived from sources as varied as the appreciation of Vermeer, Michael Jordan, Pele, Pavarotti, the sunset, children and grandchildren, an Elvis-on-velvet, a child's drawings, an evening with friends and Einstein's equations. In addition to such as these involving the natural world, I will, later, discuss happiness derived from thoughts regarding the supernatural.

There are two categories that are identified in the pursuit of happiness. One involves pursuit that is rewarding to the individual alone. The other involves the happiness and satisfaction received from doing things that directly help the group, in that the individual's actions help the group reach its goal and these same actions reward the individual with happiness. Perhaps the major area of this integration of ethics and esthetics is found in the satisfaction and happiness people receive while creating and rearing the next generation to continue the species. This is natural, as it is positive feedback received for accomplishing the primary job of perpetuation. In keeping with the functional definition of art and artists, it could be said that parents who do this job well are artists. The point is, the effort of accomplishing the group goal must be rewarded by individual happiness/satisfaction. What better way to find reward than in the direct work of raising the next generation?

There are, of course, many other ways of receiving happiness while helping the group toward the goal. Procreating but subsequently avoiding the needed work to raise the children is not helpful or ethical. Conversely, not procreating but helping in any of the thousands of ways needed to aid the group is admirably ethical. As noted earlier, passing on one's DNA does not assure perpetuation. It is clearly necessary. However, this is only one element of the whole and much more is needed for the group to perpetuate. There are many who contribute significantly to the group but, either by choice or nature, do not have children. Their happiness too must be appropriate for their contribution.

Consider the integration of esthetics and ethics in the work of artists who perform for larger numbers of group members. Some, such as sports figures, may deliver solely entertainment and produce happiness for those who appreciate the games and skills. Others, such as some comedians or singers, may use entertainment to try to influence local or world opinion. Their message is, on one level, entertaining but, in addition, they are trying to sway opinion more towards one side or the other of the liberty-equality balance inherent in all ethical systems. Thus, entertainment may overlap with the entertainer's or his employer's political message. We are so accustomed to the artist's role of opinion leader that we often ask sports artists about political issues, when their art form has nothing to do with politics.

A great orator is also an artist. There is considerable entertainment in how he or she expresses himself or herself. This talent gives him or her an advantage in the competition within the group as he or she seeks to persuade the audience of his or her ethical-political view. Art may also be used to bring attention to a particular current threat to the group or may be used as an object lesson to show how past threats were well or poorly managed. Examples are Picasso's painting inspired by the bombing of Guernica, movies and books on slavery and the Holocaust, and movies and books showing great valor and heroic deeds as citizens defend their country in war. History, in the form of pictures, movies, books or classes, may be interesting and entertaining and thus fit the functional definition of art but, in addition, it carries an ethical message of what worked for groups in the past and what did not work. It combines esthetics/art with ethics. Understanding history is the best way to avoid ethical mistakes that groups have made in the past and can give the perspective needed to recognize that some solutions to recurrent ethical problems work short term but fail in the long term.

Additionally, many derive personal happiness from individual beliefs regarding the supernatural metaphysical world. Trying to define metaphysical as nonempirical can lead to ambiguity. My more restrictive, functional definition of metaphysics is "subjective thoughts and opinions regarding things beyond the natural world." Thus, Einstein's mental image of a constantly accelerating room simulating gravity is empirically impossible but it is not metaphysical. Other knowledgeable disinterested members of the human group understand and agree with this notion and it is, therefore, objective. Since it is not a subjective thought, it is not metaphysical. The concept of God, however, is definitely subjective. This idea of a higher power deals with faith and opinion beyond the natural world, beyond what can be tested, verified or falsified. There are many knowledgeable disinterested members of the human group who do not agree with this concept. They include, for example, most of the citizens of China, a significant fraction of all Americans, and, among scientists even in America, a large majority of the members of the National Academy of Science do not agree (see Edward J. Larsen and Larry Witham's article, *Scientists and Religion in America* published in *Nature* July 1997—60 percent of scientists in general do not believe in God and 93 percent of elite scientists in the National Academy of Science do not believe in God). If one were to seek agreement regarding more specific concepts of God, such as Moslems agreeing with the Christian concept of Jesus or either group agreeing with Hindu concepts, the percent in agreement falls much lower. The concept of God is, thus, both beyond the natural world and subjective and, hence, metaphysical.

In keeping with the above definition, a synonym for metaphysics would be "supernatural." Human beings most extensive thinking regarding the metaphysical supernatural world is in the field of religion. From a practical point of view, this correlation is strong enough that religion and metaphysics can be considered synonymous. Individual belief in religion/metaphysics is the search for an ultimate reward for our effort, a bigger payoff of happiness than can be achieved in the natural world. Metaphysics/religion can be seen, then, as a subcategory of esthetics or, as some may prefer, as the ultimate extension of esthetics in the search for individual happiness. Esthetics deals with the subjective appreciation each individual has for things in both the natural world and subjective thoughts each individual has regarding the supernatural world. An individual's faith in the supernatural world and search for happiness after death is an extension of the search for pleasure, beauty, satisfaction, contentment and self-fulfillment—happiness—in the natural world. Pascal said that we are "men in chains and all condemned to death." To address this demoralizing knowledge, Pascal and many others have embraced religion. This is because it provides the vital ingredient of happiness. Functionally, philosophy's role is not to say what is beautiful or which religion (if any or all) is correct. From the point of view of ethics and getting the job done, it is important only that our happiness, from whatever sources, be sufficient to keep us working at the job and that our pursuit of happiness does not distract us from doing our primary job.

We can now see the two goals each of us has in life. There is the primary group goal of perpetuating the species and the secondary individual goal of achieving self-fulfillment—happiness. Another way to look at the same statement is to say that, other than making sure the group has the best chance of perpetuation, there is nothing more important than the individual's happiness. I would venture this theory: the happier individuals can be within the ethical limits of the group, the more efficient the group will be in its efforts toward perpetuation. Learning how to best accomplish this secondary goal can be of real value. Maslow's hierarchy may serve as a helpful guide. He described a ladder of physical needs building from physical safety, to love and belonging to a group, to self-esteem and recognition, and finally to self-actualization and self-fulfillment. Using this example, we must understand two things. The ethical needs of the group come first. Any of our individual physical or emotional needs can be sidetracked or abandoned if required by the group's goal. We must maintain our priorities. Second, if we can integrate self-fulfillment with ethical benefit for the group (deriving happiness by helping the group, which often means helping other members of the group) then we are way ahead of the game. We have achieved an ethical-esthetic "two-fer."

Now we have our paycheck, happiness, and we keep on keeping on and doing our job. If the check is insufficient, then we quit. We stop working at our job of group perpetuation. We commit suicide, or become druggies or otherwise "bail out." Such actions are not good for the group. What if we are overpaid, overly self-seeking? In a broader sense, this is the most problematic area for philosophy. We have said that it is not the role of philosophy to say what beauty or ideal form is or what should give happiness. This is an individual subjective judgment. Philosophy says that there should be enough happiness to keep us working at the job. If we get too carried away seeking our own happiness to the detriment of the group, then philosophy brands that action as unethical.

Decadence is the subtle side of unethical. It involves that category of happiness that is pursued for the individual alone rather than happiness received from helping the group. Decadence involves the loss of moderation in one's actions. It is not specific to bad art, sex or drugs. Rather, decadence is the pursuit of what are usually benign individual desires but taken to excess and, thus, detrimental to the group. These pursuits might include anything from drugs to sex to art to religion. "Excess" is not an absolute number. In times of plenty, the group may be able to afford a large percent of time for individuals to pursue personal happiness. In lean times, for example in war, there will be little time for individual pursuits. Decadence is, by definition, unethical. It is self-indulgence that creeps up on cultures. Hard work becomes less hard work becomes less work. Sex is not only critical to perpetuation but also evolved to be a major source of happiness. If, however, it becomes an all-consuming pursuit, it will, inevitably, become detrimental to the group's needs. A couple of beers in an evening may be okay but a six-pack, or more, every night may well impair the job effort. Decadence is the soft end of unethical. Crossing that line into decadence is sneaky and often subtle. It is the loss of the Greek "everything in moderation," too much of a good thing leading to unethical behavior. If we choose to quantify unethical acts on a scale, decadence would lie on the milder side, evil on the worst end. Of course, enough straws of decadence can break the camel's back and cause the group to fail. There are a myriad of examples of this from history. One generation's hard work permits the next generation to work less hard. The next generation assumes that life is about playing, happiness and self-indulgence. The empire collapses. Philosophy's job, in this regard, is to say when the line has been crossed. When less work becomes too much less, then philosophy should remind us to beware of decadence. It is time to knuckle down. There is a job to be done and don't forget it. There is an objective goal and all is dependent on that goal. It is not the action in and of itself that is decadent. Rather, decadence involves too much of the action, self-indulgence, that impairs the group's ability to accomplish the goal.

Religion can also be a source of unethical decadent behavior. We use the words "materialistic" and "materialism" to pejoratively describe decadent excesses of the secular world. Most of us have little trouble understanding that it is detrimental to the group, be it country or family, for an individual to waste his or her life with alcohol or other drugs, irresponsible sex, or other forms of excessive materialism. Yet we are less quick to recognize the problem when it applies to religion. Pursuit of happiness through religion can also lapse into decadence just as any of the more mundane individual pursuits of happiness can lapse. In fact, I suggest we use the words "maudistic" and "maudism" to reflect the problem of religious conduct lapsing into decadence. I derive it from Miss Maudie in Harper Lee's *To Kill a Mockingbird.* She said, "There are just some kind of men—who're so busy worrying about the next world they've never learned to live in this one." One can proceed into excess in the religious field just as one can fall into excess in secular areas. There is no question that religion can be and has been an indispensable aid for those of faith to help them understand and deal with the stresses of the natural world. It has often provided relief from suffering—improvement in the negative side of happiness—giving sufficient reward or balm to enable individuals to continue on with life in spite of severe stresses. It can also provide happiness for individuals, even when there is no particular stress. Religion can thus provide tangible benefits for the individual as well as for the group by helping them continue the job effort for the group. However, one can get so involved in religion that it impairs one's ability to do one's job in the natural world. It can be a decadent excuse for doing less work for the group when more work is needed. Then a person becomes a burden. They do not contribute as they ethically need to for the group. Whether it is personal material pursuit in excess or personal religious pursuit in excess, the result is the same—decadence. Decadence may be the soft end of unethical behavior but, nonetheless, whether materialistic or maudistic, it is unethical since it impairs the group's ability to accomplish the goal.

Decadence, or worse, may also arise when the internal rules of a religion are at variance with the overall needs of the group. Angst appears when we must label decadent or unethical the situation in which an individual interprets his or her religious code as requiring one approach while the larger group's needs require a different approach. Unethical, including decadence, is, however, an objective label. Catering to individual desires to the detriment of the group's goal is, by definition, unethical. Holding religious convictions does not make one's actions any less unethical. Concepts derived from religion are not exempt from ethical standards. Birth control and nonviolence are examples of this. If the larger group is threatened by having too many people, it may be determined that birth control is needed. Then it is decadent, or worse, for individuals to continue producing more children. Similarly, it may be difficult and uncomfortable to label as decadent, or worse, a heartfelt commitment to pacifism, when war is needed to preserve the larger group. Nonetheless, with an objective goal, such actions are self-indulgent and fit the definition of decadent and unethical.

The fundamental problem of unethical behavior, whether by religious maudism or secular materialism, is one of the individual indulging his or her personal desire for happiness to the detriment of the group. It is excess selfishness and egotism, putting your wants, whether material or metaphysical, ahead of the group's needs. It is forgetting, or ignoring, that the group goal comes first. Politics can be a headline example of unethical behavior. The dark side of politics is the same as other unethical behavior; an individual indulges or benefits himself or his subgroup to the detriment of the larger group. Members join the larger group because of the advantages afforded to them. They assume the obligation to ensure the larger group can accomplish its primary goal and to place this group goal first. Politics becomes unethical when individual politicians have an uncontrollable desire to benefit themselves to the detriment of the larger group. These excesses occur frequently enough for the words "politics" and "politician" to have definite negative connotations and for politics itself to have earned its own vocabulary reflecting this unethical behavior: nepotism, cronyism, pork barrel spending, etc.

Philosophy makes no statement about the correctness or incorrectness of metaphysics-religion. Faith and belief are words used to describe acceptance of a particular religious-metaphysical concept. The concepts are individual and subjective and not usable by the group as a whole. However, we are all existentialists. That is, we all seek to explain to ourselves the reason for our existence. We each seek Kierkegaard's "truth that is true for me." While we may all be existentialists seeking a subjective truth, we are also all agnostics when we look to the supernatural for answers. The most fervent of the faithful and the most adamant of the atheists are in the same subjective, intellectual boat. There are no objective facts regarding the supernatural. Most beliefs and faiths regarding the supernatural fall somewhere between Kierkegaard and Sartre—between reason-suspended, mystical faith in the Divine and reason-based atheism that assumes we are each alone. These beliefs can form a base on which we build our own explanation for human existence. So long as these beliefs work for each of us without hurting the larger group, then all is well. Yet, it is critical to understand the proper sequence that must be followed. Alyosha's (Dostoevsky's) point contained in the quote at the beginning of the Starting Assumption is the key: we must love life more than the meaning of life. It is the needs of the group as a whole first, the needs of the individual second—secular before religious. If religious individuals and groups understand this sequencing, then humans can have a much better chance at having both group perpetuation and individual pursuit of religion. If, on the other hand, religious individuals and subgroups place their goals above all else, detrimental conflicts can arise. The religious individuals would be, by definition, unethical in placing their supernatural goal ahead of group perpetuation. The most worrisome concern is that many religions look to life after death as their reward. In pursuing a goal that can be achieved only after death, some religious individuals can thus justify elimination of natural life. By reversing the proper order of priorities, religion can endanger the fulfillment of the primary job, perpetuation, much to the detriment of the whole of humanity.

    Is religion the "opiate of the masses"? Yes, it is. But then, so is a conversation with friends, golf, reading, walking in the woods, camel racing, hunting, art, ballet, etc. Anything that gives us pleasure, our generic term happiness, could be described as an opiate.

It is what keeps us working at the group's objective job. Religion, as a major source of happiness for many, is then one of the opiates. Marx used this phrase in a pejorative manner, implying that it kept the masses repressed. He, no doubt, regarded himself as an atheist. He, of course, was really an agnostic like the rest of us. He knew no more about the supernatural than the rest of us. Philosophy doesn't have anything specific to say about whether religion is good or bad for a group. It could be either and has been both. Philosophy says that we need to get the secular goal right first and that religion cannot hamper that goal. If religion can help, by providing happiness, then it can be good. If it hinders the group by resisting needed changes or by impairing needed group formation, then it can be bad. Ethically speaking, religion is good or bad only in whether it helps or hinders the group in striving toward its goal.

This discussion of these two elements, esthetics and metaphysics, completes our functional structure of philosophy. We have our most important function of perpetuation of the species. This is the goal, the necessary common frame of reference, the first premise, the greatest good. We gather objective data and process it into objective cause and effect theories. Working as a group, we use these theories to direct our conduct, ethics, along paths most likely to permit us to accomplish our goal. Each individual uses the same objective data, plus such subjective data as appeals to him or her, to formulate subjective theories to direct personal conduct to enable him or her to have happiness—the individual's reward while working within the group. Individuals can be unethical by continuing to pursue their own happiness when such pursuit is detrimental to the group. Groups can be unethical by not protecting their members, by interfering with their members' pursuit of happiness, or by not permitting equal opportunity for their members to compete. The group's conduct is limited in these obligations because the group may not ethically do anything that will impair its ability to pursue perpetuation. Thus, there can be ethical exceptions to the obligations.

The most problematic area for philosophy involves individuals seeking personal happiness to the detriment of the larger group. We understand the priority of the group over the individual. Yet, this prioritization seems awkward when individual subjective belief, faith and ostensibly good intentions are pitted against group objective needs. We can help resolve this awkwardness by recognizing the differences between ethics for the group and morals for the individual. Thus we come to the next section—understanding the difference between ethics and morals.

UNDERSTANDING THE DIFFERENCE BETWEEN ETHICS AND MORALS

"It is only singular institutions which thus confound laws, manners, and customs—things naturally distinct and separate; but though they are in themselves different, there is nevertheless a great relation between them."
—Montesquieu, *The Spirit of Laws*

"What is new, however, is always evil, being that which wants to conquer and overthrow the old boundary markers and the old pieties; and only what is old is good."
—Friedrich Nietzsche, *The Gay Science*

The *bête-noire* of ethics is the urge each of us has to fulfill our individual desire for happiness, even if this is detrimental to the group's ability to accomplish its primary goal. To act on these urges is unethical. If, however, we think that this urge is justified by our view of morals, it becomes the source of most philosophical-ethical dichotomies. The problem (and the solution) of these moral-ethical dichotomies is best understood by examining how ethics and morals differ. I will start with a simple chart.

ETHICS	*MORALS*
Group	Individual
Uses objective data	Uses subjective data
Forward thinking in time	Past thinking in time
Flexible	Rigid
Realistic	Idealistic

Ethics is premised on the assumption that nothing is more important than the group's primary goal of perpetuation of the group/species. Regardless of whatever else happens, our conduct (ethics) must not impair the group's ability to accomplish this goal. Morals and mores come from the same Latin word, *mos,* meaning custom. Morals, true to its origins, are based on customs. Customs and morals reflect the rules that the group has historically utilized. In effect, today's morals are yesterday's ethics. There is, therefore, considerable overlap between moral rules and current ethical rules. Often, in history, the threats and resources of a group have remained static for long periods of time, encompassing multiple generations. Under these circumstances, the ethical rules and the moral rules merge and are essentially identical. Dichotomies and problems arise when the times change and the threats, stresses and environment of the group change. To accommodate changes, ethics must be flexible to assure perpetuation of the group. At least some of the ethical rules must change. What might have been moral and ethical yesterday becomes unethical today. If the group becomes ossified around yesterday's ethics, which have become group customs and morals, then there can be disastrous consequences. Failure of the group to change when needed could result in elimination, the ultimate unethical behavior. (With an objective goal, ethical theories are testable. Elimination of a group constitutes falsification of an ethical theory.) A group can never forget its primary goal, and it must change its ethical rules when necessary to give itself the best chance of perpetuation.

Changing some of the ethical rules does not mean you need to change all of them. You don't "throw out the baby with the bath water." As we have seen, the secondary ethical rules, addressing group formation and efficient function, remain stable for thousands of years. For example, the Confucian virtues, courtesy, tolerance, good faith, diligence and generosity, are still valid. Ethical rules that still have an appropriate function, those that are still working, are left intact.

Primary ethical rules, however, are very likely to require adjustments and changes since they must directly respond to changes in resources, the environment, composition of the group, the role of women within the group, population requirements, etc. These are the areas where new and better information will produce better theories and falsify older theories. An example is the need for varying responses to issues regarding population including over- and underpopulation and imbalances in the numbers of males versus females. Too few men in a small group that needs more members makes it ethical for a man to have more than one wife. With an overly large population, this same behavior can be unethical. The need for high birth rates to replace a population constantly devastated by diseases makes birth control unethical, yet, overpopulation makes not using birth control unethical. Combinations can and have varied. It is easy to see how individuals can identify with yesterday's population problems and conclude that yesterday's actions are moral and should not be changed. For the group, however, if a new theory is shown to be valid, then it is unethical not to change, even if some individuals consider this immoral. This may be seen in other areas, particularly with environmental resources, but nowhere is the misunderstanding of ethics and morals more apparent than in how we control our human population. Seeing birth control as immoral, in an age of overpopulation, is an example of ossifying around yesterday's ethics. It is as out of place as continuing to insist that the earth is the center of the universe. Contemporary China represents an excellent example of this ethical necessity. The government has disincentives for a family to have more than one child and this is correct ethics given their population. In today's world, few if any places are underpopulated. Thus, failure to recommend birth control is unethical. The world group, today, cannot allow people to hide behind their individual morals while turning a blind eye toward the implications of overpopulation. Ethics must consider future generations as well as the current generation and must consider the impact on the group as more important than the impact on the individual. Individual morals, based on custom, may indulge in the luxury of being fixed in the past, focused on individuals and not taking responsibility for the objective goal of the group. Ethics, for the group, cannot afford to do this.

Religion/metaphysics represents a particularly effective method of making morals more rigid by utilizing both past ethics and subjective data. Thus, it represents a particular problem when circumstances change. The morals developed by a culture are integrated with the culture's religion. The process starts with a set of ethical rules developed by a particular group at a particular time in history. Commonly, these pragmatic rules integrate with revelation from a supernatural deity. Efficient, appropriate rules permit the group to have tangible success, while groups with inadequate or inappropriate rules are eliminated. In time, the rules of a surviving group then become codified into supernatural divine decree. From that point on, the rules then attempt to maintain the culture of the past regardless of the changing circumstances. The original, pragmatic rules are now based in the supernatural, and, therefore, they cannot effectively be criticized or changed by using objective data from the natural world. They are, so to speak, the "rules of God." Even these rules may eventually change as, for example, the position of the Christian religion on slavery did. However, when trying to change to accommodate to new threats, groups usually face high levels of inertia, regardless of objective data presented. This situation places science at odds with religion. Science provides the objective data and theories for the natural world. When information improves or otherwise changes, as it inevitably does, science will, relatively quickly, change theories. These new theories can then be used to develop new ethics. Religions that espouse unchanging truths will be particularly slow to acknowledge new data and to implement needed new theories. Subjective, religious data is personal. It is not necessarily subject to change regardless of objective data. It does not have to be verifiable or falsifiable. In addition, any change in the theories and the ethical rules could be perceived as weakening the religious/metaphysical foundation on which the happiness of religious individuals depends. Religious individuals will, therefore, consider change as having a negative impact on the validity of their beliefs and will resist change. Religion is thus a two-edged sword with both short-term and long-term implications. The short-term advantage of religion is well known. It is useful in maintaining a stable group by providing rules and a supernatural policeman. Yet, long term, religion can create a situation of unchangeable rules, some of which are no longer effective in giving the group the best chance of perpetuation. In this case, short-term moral and ethical rules become long-term moral but unethical rules. Individuals can remain moral in their own minds and actions by not accepting new data or theories. However, they will become unethical if their actions do not support the group goal of perpetuation.

As I discussed earlier, there is no question that religion has value and importance. It provides the needed happiness and reward for much of humanity. This reward is a necessity in the group's overall ability to accomplish the primary goal. However, we must assign the correct priorities to individual actions. Ethics for the group, by virtue of the group's primary goal, is more important than morals for the individual. If a dichotomy arises, then ethics comes first. The problem is between the subjective desires of individuals of the current generation for happiness—esthetics—and the long-term objective need of the group for survival—ethics. Religion is cited specifically because, of all the areas that provide individuals happiness, there is none more important to more people than religion. Because it is the area most important to many individuals, it is also the area where individuals are most likely to be inflexible and to, thereby, convince themselves to act unethically. Hence, religion has frequently provided justification for the worst unethical behavior.

Understanding the difference between ethics and morals enables us to eliminate the confusion involved with relativism and cultural relativism. James Rachels has a concise discussion of the problem in his book *The Elements of Moral Philosophy*. The problem of relativism is based on this observation: "Different cultures have different moral codes." The problems raised by this observation can be resolved by understanding the distinction between ethics and morals. Once we understand this, then we will agree that different societies can and do have different moral codes. Indeed, the moral code of our society is merely one among many. However, this is not to say that an ethical code is merely one among many. The terms moral and ethical are not synonymous. Relativism applies to moral codes, which are the customs from the past very likely related to "yesterday's ethics." If not unethical, morals or customs can be retained by the group indefinitely. The term relativism, when used regarding the retained morals and customs, implies arbitrary inclusion. Customs may seem arbitrary to individuals outside of the group who have different traditions, but these moral customs aid internal group maintenance, much as the secondary ethical rules of the virtues do for virtually all groups. While there is no universal truth among the wide variety of retained customs and morals, there is a universal truth of sorts for ethics—the goal of perpetuation of the group/species. This objective frame of reference takes the arbitrary connotation out of ethics. If ethics varies between groups it is because the stresses and threats imposed on the group vary, not because of cultural differences. We can now understand one of Rachels's relativism examples: why in times of scarce resources the Eskimos could ethically condone infanticide while Americans, with no similar resource problem, cannot. It has nothing to do with relativism as usually discussed. The moral distaste for infanticide is most likely the same for each group. The different situations necessitate different responses, but the response of each group is ethically appropriate to the objective goal. Rachels alludes to this pragmatism when he states, *"there are some moral rules that all societies will have in common, because these rules are necessary for society to exist."* (Rachels's italics) Problems occur when Rachels fails to separate morals and ethics. Thus, his quote would be absolutely correct if he changed his word *morals* to *ethics* and acknowledged the distinction between the two terms.

It is a deontological prohibition that if an individual's or subgroup's customs and morals are not unethical and they are presumably promoting happiness within the subgroup, then it is unethical for the larger group to interfere. Thus, we should be extremely wary of labeling "immoral" the personal actions of others in the realms of sex and religion. Getting on a moral "high horse" is most likely not defensible in terms of ethics. Further, it is also potentially unethical if it negatively affects group functioning. If we start throwing moral stones, we may find that each of us lives in a glass house that somebody in the group will label immoral. Accepting that restriction, however, does not keep us from labeling some customs/morals as unethical. Ethical behavior is based on objective evaluation of how the response worked in perpetuating the group. If customs/morals are inappropriate to that end, then they are unethical.

The major distinguishing factor between moral and ethical theories is that moral theories use subjective data. John Rawls's *A Theory of Justice* is an important example of a moral theory. It is helpful to examine this theory briefly as Rawls raises questions and offers challenges in his defense of a subjective intuitive approach. In a Kantian approach, this theory relies on our intuition to play a key role in the formation of a theory of justice. A priori and intuitive data have been accepted historically as objective and, hence, have been used to develop ethical theories. However, after the last century, with the improved concept of verifiable, followed by Popper's further improvements of the requirements of testable and falsifiable, it is highly unlikely that intuitive data would be accepted as objective today. Thus, theories based on intuition are no longer acceptable as a basis for ethical theories. Regarding this intuitive approach Rawls states, "The only way therefore to dispute intuitionism is to set forth the recognizably ethical criteria that account for the weights which, in our considered judgments, we think appropriate to give to the plurality of principles." Further, he states, "Intuitionism denies that there exists any useful explicit solution to the priority problem." Basing our lives on perpetuation of the species provides such a priority and a way to weight our principles—and to do so objectively. This book's elaboration of ethics based on perpetuation of the species represents a "systematic account" of how such an ethical theory works. The priority of perpetuation of the species is the explicit overriding objective end that becomes the needed common frame of reference necessary to adjudicate a system of justice as it forms a component of an ethical system. Such a common frame of reference, an objective first premise, is lacking in all intuitive, subjective theories, including *A Theory of Justice*. Thus, these intuitive theories may be useful as individual moral theories but are not acceptable as group ethical theories.

In general, moral theories may be regarded as secondary ethical theories. This is because they tend to deal with the secondary deontological rules of ethics involving group formation and maintenance. The real problem comes in understanding the exceptions that ethics forces on moral theories. Just as there is much agreement between morals and ethics, there is also much agreement between a moral theory of justice and the ethical theory of perpetuation. The ethical theory of perpetuation would agree that, as Rawls says, justice is the first virtue of social institutions and a public conception of justice does constitute the fundamental character of a well-ordered human association. *But,* ethically speaking, the reason for this is that a well-ordered association is a vital component of the secondary ethical rules needed for the group to give itself the best chance of perpetuation. Justice, which provides protection for individual members, is a fundamental obligation of the group for its *accepted* members but, as we have noted, justice and the other secondary ethical rules can be withheld even from accepted members if this is necessary to ensure the group's perpetuation. There is also agreement that justice has a role in determining distributive shares, which affects the efficiency, coordination and stability of the group. In the ethical theory, how those shares are best distributed is ultimately determined by the usefulness of such distribution in contributing to the group's goal of perpetuation, and not primarily by how it affects the individual members.

The two theories agree that equal opportunity does not depend on social circumstances of members. Both acknowledge equal rights of members regarding opportunity and protection. Both would have people of uncommon ability able to move upward in the governance scheme of the group. In fact, the ethical theory would very likely be more adamant that talent moves up. Here again we see a difference in reasons why that is required. For the moral theory it is more for the benefit of the individual, and a talented individual could decide that, for personal reasons of happiness, he or she does not want the additional responsibility or work. Ethically speaking, members do not have the right to withhold their talent from the group. The ethical theory requires that the most talented members move upward in the governance scheme to where they can help the group the most. The ethical theory needs to give equal opportunity to all members to ensure that it can identify the best talent among group members; the effect on the individual is of secondary importance.

Rawls's theory of justice is based on being fair to the individual and bringing more benefit to more individuals. Rawls would say that justice and fairness do not represent a maximizing notion. I would agree but would phrase it differently. A system based on subjective/intuitive, individual benefits can indulge in the luxury of not specifying what consequence such a theory will yield. These systems may give a glimpse of long-term consequences, but they have a great tendency to be primarily concerned with short-term consequences for the current generation. They will accept a so-called realm of ends/consequences long term for the group. An objective ethical theory based on perpetuation requires maximizing the chances the group has of both short-term survival and long-term perpetuation. It is indeed a maximizing theory. It will accept no other possibility out of the realm of ends. Justice is important in helping to ensure that goal, but it is a tool. Its importance is in the impact it has on the group, not primarily in how it affects the individual. This yields further divergence, since acknowledging the advantage of members with increased talent for aiding perpetuation means all members are not of equal importance to the group. In some circumstances, those of more value are treated preferentially. All moral theories, including Rawls's theory of justice, are subject to restrictions imposed on them by the necessity of maximizing the group's chance of survival and perpetuation. Ethics cannot live in the academic ivory tower. In an ideal world, justice/morals could merge with the real world of ethics. Ethics, however, must live in the real world of objective theories. It is interesting to note that Thomas More's *Utopia* was written in Latin and originally titled *Nusquama,* which means nowhere. While it is of practical, objective necessity that there be considerable agreement between the theory of justice for the individual and the ethical theory of perpetuation for the group, many of the reasons for agreement will be different, and exceptions will be required under the priority of the ethical theory of perpetuation. Rawls, on the first page of *A Theory of Justice,* states that "Each person possesses an inviolability founded on justice that even the welfare of society as a whole cannot override. . . . It does not allow that the sacrifices imposed on a few are outweighed by the larger sum of advantages enjoyed by the many." The ethical theory of perpetuation disagrees with that premise. Ethical theory would say that innocents usually are not to be sacrificed, *but* it would weigh the advantages and disadvantages of how such a sacrifice would affect the group's goal accomplishment. If the judgment based on the available objective data dictated that sacrificing the individual would advance the likelihood of perpetuation, as in the case of Eskimo infanticide, then it is ethically required.

It is worth noting again that a smoothly functioning group requires that the tenets of justice be present and enforced. This is an area where intent does, indeed, make a difference. We discussed earlier that intention is irrelevant for ethics with an objective goal. For justice, however, intention is an inescapable vital feature of considerable importance. Perfect ethics does not exist because there are no perfect objective cause and effect theories. There will inevitably be unethical behavior, some that is intentional and some that is unintentional. Justice is needed to sort these out and to appropriately reward and punish members in order to maintain the most efficient, smoothly functioning group. The ethical theory of perpetuation has justice as a tool needed for efficient group functioning. The better it is, the more smoothly the group will work towards its goal. It helps to accomplish the goal of the group, not primarily to protect the individual. Usually protecting the individual will be in the best interest of the group. It is a vital, recognized part of the deontological system of mutual obligations between the individual and the group. We must realize, however, that if protecting the individual jeopardizes the group then the individual loses out.

Rawls's theory of justice does acknowledge that injustice to an individual can be sanctioned if it avoids a greater injustice. Therefore, what if a theory of justice used this definition, "the greatest injustice would be to not perpetuate the species"? Then, the theory could justify individual injustice if it would be required to avoid the greater injustice of not perpetuating the species. That one objective definition of the greatest injustice would transform the theory of justice to a maximizing theory. It would maximize the avoidance of the greatest injustice. It would be the double negative form of the ethical theory of perpetuation, and would no longer be a subjective, moral theory. The primary objective goal would be perpetuation and injustice to the individual would have to be accepted when required to avoid the greatest injustice of nonperpetuation.

The distinction between ethical theories and moral theories is not just academic. The devil is not in the details. The difference is fundamental. Ethical theory must deal with what is objectively best for the group. As stated in the introduction, you and I and the preponderance of our human group must agree on the starting point if we are to concur with the conclusions. No matter how erudite the structure, if we do not agree with the initial position—the foundation on which the structure is built—then it is all a house of cards. Subjective moral starting points create erroneous conclusions. Such is the case with the notion that all humans are ethically equal and other animals are ethically equal to humans. Equality is a luxury of the subjective concepts involved in esthetics and metaphysics/religion, but not in ethics and politics. It is also erroneous to conclude that the most important result is to produce an unusually talented superman. This position is an extension of a subjective individual moral theory advocating liberty over equality. The error of each position has to be identified at page one. If that initial, subjective position is permitted to slip by unnoticed and unchallenged, then what follows, while seeming reasonable, is faulty.

We each have our own morals. Fortunately, most of our moral rules overlap with the ethical rules of the group as a whole. If this were not the case, it would be difficult for the group to exist. It is critical, then, to understand the places where they do not overlap. We have a prototype in the writings of Machiavelli, although he has to be read as giving advice to the group and not just to an individual prince. The book we would use today would be an updated version of Machiavelli's works, titled something like *The Ethical Restrictions Imposed on Theories of Moral Philosophy and Justice.* Exceptions that invariably occur in individual-based moral inductive theories do not make the rule. Rather, they impose on us the obligation to seek better theories that also accommodate the exceptions.

Ethics deals with group-based objective reality, while morals deal with individual-based subjective idealism. Often, morals make use of subjective religious concepts. Ethics, which deals with reality, uses the verb "to be." Morals, which deal with idealism, uses conditional verbs such as "ought to be" and "should be." Ethics must be flexible in order to accomplish the goal. Morals can be rigid, with either no goal or an indefinite, untestable subjective goal.

I suspect it could be argued that most moral theories, including the contractual ones, are classical utilitarian theories ultimately based on individual happiness. Labeling a theory utilitarian is not, of course, a negative. Indeed, the whole point of philosophy is to be useful or utilitarian, and particularly for a theory based on perpetuation of the species. Any approach to ethics has to be useful. Otherwise why bother with the theory? The only real question is whether it is primarily useful for the individual or primarily useful for the group. Ethics based on perpetuation of the species is objective and deductive and can be judgmental and, thus, useful, primarily for the group. All actions and theories are judged as to how well they contribute to achieving the group goal. The goal is not arbitrary. Individual members must agree with the goal of group perpetuation. This ethical theory appreciates that without individual happiness there will be no work towards the goal and the goal achievement will fail. This theory takes both the goal and individual happiness into consideration, but it never doubts which has priority. Kant can certainly say that life without justice is not worth living. However, it must be recognized that this is his personal position as to what gives him happiness. Justice, for him, is what makes his life worth living. Yet, as important as justice is for group maintenance, it is not as important as survival of the group and it cannot be the primary basis for ethics. The group's goal is always more important than an individual's desire for happiness. The theory of perpetuation is unwilling to accept an unknown realm of ends, which means that, at times, it is necessary to violate a person's moral beliefs in favor of the group's ethics.

Ethics and morals represent the two, sometimes conflicting, intertwined themes of human existence: the group's primary need for perpetuation versus the individual's desire for happiness. The group is more important than the individual and, thus, ethics trumps morals. In the section to follow, we will consider some specific ethical-moral questions and make judgments as to the correct answers based on this prioritization. Here, understanding the difference between ethics and morals will be most helpful. It will help us recognize that each question actually has two parts, one based on ethics and one based on morals. Since the answer will be restricted by the prioritized ethics of the situation, it is almost a surety that some of the answers derived will offend how each of us thinks things ought to be, our moral view of the problem. We may not like the answers. Still, we will have to accept them because they support the most important goal. If avoiding human extinction is our top priority, then ethics always takes priority over morals.

THE JUDGMENTAL ROLE OF PHILOSOPHY

THE PRIORITIZATION AND INTEGRATION OF THE GROUP'S NEEDS WITH THE INDIVIDUAL'S PURSUIT OF HAPPINESS

> "... anyone who abandons what is for what should be pursues his own downfall rather than his preservation."
> —Niccolo Machiavelli, *The Prince*

We cannot be deluded into thinking that because we feel a situation *should be* a certain way that it actually is. We have to deal with objective reality. Machiavelli's advice quoted above, that if we abandon *what is* for what *should be* then we pursue our own downfall, applies. The judgments will be based on the deductive ethical theory we developed, the basis of which is that nothing is more important than perpetuation of the group/species. Start with the example of the overloaded lifeboat. The situation is this: a lifeboat in stormy seas can handle only 20 people but there are 25 who have crawled in. The boat will sink if all 25 stay on board, so what should be done? This is an example demonstrating that, ethically speaking, all members of a group are not equal. Those capable of rowing the boat to shore must be saved in preference to some of the weaker less capable people. What combination of 20 out of the 25 gives the best chance of 20 survivors—group survival? It would be unethical to keep more than 20 since it would jeopardize the survival of the whole group. Strategically speaking, first chosen are the strong rowers, then perhaps someone with navigational skills. The final choice, among those left, will be based on who is most useful once on shore. The older, the handicapped and anyone likely to be a burden are among those that go over the side. It may be uncomfortable, for some unjust and immoral. Nonetheless, it is ethical and it deals with reality.

Let's now look at the reverse of the overloaded lifeboat with a theoretical problem for world humanity. There is to be a monumental plague or an asteroid impact or other unavoidable calamity to affect the earth. We have a three-months' warning. Fortunately, a space station is ready with transportation for 200 people. All humans who do not depart to the space station will die. After two years, the earth will again be habitable by humans. Then the 200 from the space station will be able to restart the human race. No frozen sperm or eggs can be accommodated. Who do you ethically choose to be among the 200?

The first thing to realize is that we don't want to draw straws. The second thing to realize is that we must choose the group carefully. No 60-year-old philosophers are going to be on board. Nor will the crew include politicians, handicapped, infertile people, homosexuals, people with health problems, medical subspecialists, Wall Street financial experts, lawyers or religious fanatics. These are less valuable types. Set up the conditions as you like for what will be left on earth to work with when the 200 return. Those conditions will then determine whom you choose. When perpetuation of the species clearly rests on the 200, we quickly see that we are not ethically equal. The 200 are our only hope. They need to be the best we have at the moment. Money, influence, power and the other rewards that, presumably, indicate currently talented members, successful in group competition to handle previous problems, have little ethical bearing on these new completely different circumstances. It would be unethical to choose those who will survive for any reason other than fertility and filling the predicted needs of the group of 200—humanity's only hope. In all probability, farmers, mechanics, one or two general medical doctors, engineers and others with practical professional skills would offer the most advantage. In all probability, the chosen population would include more women than men, for reproductive purposes. In the same vein, genetic diversity would be high on the list of important attributes.

Showing how the details would work out is an interesting exercise, but I will leave that to Stephen King or Steven Spielberg. For our purposes, this example is useful because it points out the folly of trying to consider that everyone is ethically equal or that everyone has equal value to the group. It is only the individual, working with subjective goals or means involving esthetics, metaphysics/religion and morals, who can indulge in the luxury of considering everybody as equal. This approach is not ethically tenable since it marginalizes the group's primary goal. Subjective approaches represent wrongheaded thinking. While they are in error, they are common in writings about ethics. In this particular situation, if you ignore the necessity of the primary goal you would very likely lose the human race entirely. This hypothetical situation also makes clear that the presence or absence of other animals is reasonably considered only in regard to how they would help or hurt the survival of the human race. Clearly, other animals are not equal in terms of human ethical considerations. They can be important for other secondary reasons including human happiness, usefulness, and environmental protection, but they are not equal in ethical considerations.

As an aside, this group of 200 would probably come to use a generic term such as "earthlings" to refer to themselves. The heritage of each would be known, but there would be no advantage to being considered a Russian earthling or an American earthling or a Chinese earthling. Such a reference might well be divisive, insinuating that a particular heritage or previous subgroup membership was more important than the fact they were the only remaining earthlings. In a similar fashion I suggest that we are mistaken in terms of group coherence here in America to refer to ourselves by first listing our ethnic subgroup. I suggest we would be better off by leading with our ace and calling ourselves Americans, rather than African Americans, Asian Americans, Irish Americans, etc. I suggest that a better system is to use the ethnic designation as a trailing modifier following American, if used at all. Thus a person would be an American of Asian heritage or an American of African heritage. American is the important common feature and, if listed first, would help to emphasize that we are all in this together as one group and not as divisive separate entities. The fact that the phrase an American of Arab heritage is more awkward to say could serve to encourage the dropping of the ethnic background designation. Then, such descriptors might be reserved for the few situations where it might be needed, such as in medical history or for identification of an unknown person.

Before we leave this particular ethical problem, let us note that the group of 200 also demonstrates to us the practical benefit of the secondary ethical rules, the virtues, as applied to group maintenance. Such virtues as honesty, justice, compassion and keeping promises would almost always be ethical. How could the group function well without incorporating these qualities? Within the well-defined group of 200, we can readily see the advantage of "do unto others . . . " as a necessary group preservative. The virtues are granted their well-deserved ethical status because of their considerable value in promoting group maintenance and efficiency, thereby aiding the group in accomplishing its goal.

I would hope that it does not require an impending disaster on the scale outlined above to make the world recognize that we are all in this together. It would be much more efficient to solve the world's primary ethical problems as one group. It would also afford much more individual happiness throughout the world. It would be nice to treat everyone the same with regard to the secondary ethical rules, even as the 200 earthlings must do to survive. We are not there yet. Machiavelli understood the weaknesses of divided city-states, which allowed them to be continually overrun by larger powers. Although he was not listened to in his time, this caused him to advocate the unification of Italy. The world has a similar problem. Our threats are global. If we fail to unite as a cohesive larger group, we do so at our own peril. We would do well to remember that ignoring threats is fundamentally unethical. Hence, working toward a single world group is ethical since this manner of organization offers us, and the rest of the world, the best chance for perpetuation. Until we unite, however, all groups will need good defenses and don't expect that the other groups will necessarily tell you the truth.

This brings us to the question of ethics and war. The subject can be better approached as "ethical" war rather than the more commonly used "just" war. The concept of a "just" war is based on subjective, individual concepts and tenets. This is essentially the same issue that was considered in the Ethics–Morals section, which addressed justice as a moral theory and not an ethical theory. Just as justice and other moral constructs are usually (but not always) ethical so the bases for a "just" war are usually (but not always) ethical. "Just" war restrictions, like restrictions imposed on justice by ethics, are inappropriate if they benefit the individual but are detrimental to the group. Without the objective frame of reference, the concept of a "just" war is uneven and applied by personal opinion. In fact, the personal opinion of some would say that war is always unjust.

The essence of "just" war theories or "ethical" war theories can be broken down into two aspects: the first has to do with determining whether waging war is worth it to the group—when is it appropriate to go to war; the second has to do with how to limit civilian damage—how much force to use in managing the war. The problem with trying to limit civilian casualties is illustrated by Winston Churchill in his book *Their Finest Hour*. He writes, "In total war it is quite impossible to draw any precise lines between military and nonmilitary problems." Even those that agree that war is sometimes "just" have difficulty sorting the civilians from the guerrillas and discussing when "collateral damage" is acceptable. The basic difficulty with the civilian aspect of a "just" war concept is that it tries to protect the individual when the conflict is between groups and not between individuals. If "civilians" are members of the group at war, they will be part of the collateral damage and such action is not unethical. This was true with the southerners "trampled" by Sherman's march across the south and, I judge, true of the use of the atom bomb on Japan at the end of World War II. It is important to recognize that preserving "civilians" of the opposing group is not the primary goal. Thus, restrictions against harming "civilians" cannot be ethically permitted if such restrictions would impair the war effort.

Still, gratuitous violence that does not advance the cause of accomplishing the ethical goal is unethical. Under the older (and still extant) Darwin/Spencer survival-of-the-fittest variation for perpetuation of the species, groups have been able to ethically justify some very harsh and lethal actions against other groups in war. Yet today, assuming that a single world group is the preferred approach to the problem of perpetuation, it would most likely be best in war to leave a country intact so it can become a positively contributing member of the world community/group. Transition to a single world unit will be easier if the winners have dealt lightly with the losers, using as little force as possible. The answer to how much force is ethical depends on why there was sufficient threat or advantage to the group that it chose war in the first place. Once it has been determined that war is necessary, the group uses the amount of force that gives it the best opportunity of being able to accomplish its goal, not only in the short term but also in the long term. It is the long-term requirement of ethics that today makes it extremely likely that the least *effective* force and attendant destruction is probably best.

When is it appropriate to go to war? When is war ethical? The answer is the same as the answer to any question about ethics. That which is ethical is based on objective data and the best objective theories for group perpetuation. There is no ethical requirement that the opponent throw the first punch. There is an ethical requirement that the data and theories correctly analyze the threat, and that war is determined to be the best of the possible solutions. The theories recommending war must always consider the long-term consequences. In so doing, many of the concepts prevalent in "just" war will also prove valid for ethical war, even as there is considerable overlap between morals and ethics. War is a means. Neither war nor avoidance of war is the goal. We understand that war is expensive to the group. It uses up both valuable individuals and resources that the group could well need for other constructive purposes addressing other threats and needs. But accomplishment of our primary goal is what we cannot lose sight of, and we need to use whatever means is best suited for the problem we encounter and those means include war as well as peace.

Religion can be a particular problem as a cause for war. As we discussed, religions usually base their beliefs on unchangeable "truths." The validity of the religion for many individuals becomes inextricably linked to not accepting any change that might seem to threaten their tenets. In accommodating new circumstances, the secular world may make needed changes slowly, but in comparison to religious groups, the secular world can turn on a dime. Galileo and Copernicus' heliocentric theory of the solar system versus the Catholic Church's entrenched earth-centered position is a good example. Slavery in the secular world versus the world of Islam is another example. Unchangeable "truths" of religion will thus often come into conflict with the necessary changing "truths" of the secular world. Here we see the basis for the conflict between religion and science. Science is part of philosophy. It is the term we give to objective epistemological data and theories used by the secular world to develop ethics for the group. Religion is for the individual and uses subjective data, faith, to confirm its position. There are two problems that come from choosing to deal with life based on subjective, individual ideals rooted in unchanging "truths." The first problem is how to deal with the new data and theories. This problem is allied to changing moral customs around the world. The traditional method of management is to ignore or forcibly suppress the information. With worldwide communication, this approach is now much less effective. The second problem is that the religious groups will inevitably find themselves at a competitive disadvantage in the secular world against groups that can adjust theories to deal with changing reality.

These problems, resulting from being less able to adjust, create significant stress between religious groups and secular groups. The stress created by new data and decreased competitiveness can be perceived as a threat to the religious group's goal—preserving the religion. When maintaining a religion is the primary goal of a group, and that group feels the goal is threatened, they may feel justified in using lethal force. In fact, with Buddhism as an exception, war is a time-honored tradition used to protect and expand religious groups. For example, the three currently dominant monotheistic religions all draw on the same militant origins from the Old Testament. As cited in Karen Armstrong's *A History of God,* Yahweh proved himself worthy of being the god of the Jews (and thus eventually also of Christians and Moslems) by being successful in war—". . . a god of war, who would be known as Yahweh Sabaoth, the God of Armies. . . . Yahweh had proved his expertise in war . . . " Religious groups, particularly fundamental religious groups, see themselves as ethical (actually moral) and have no difficulty validating war against other religious groups or secular groups if they think they perceive a threat to their religion. Even human survival and perpetuation can become a secondary goal for members of religious groups who believe the ultimate goal may be realized only after death. This is a chilling concern in an age of weapons of mass destruction.

In the secular world, there are at least two provisos that must be followed when waging war. First, weapons cannot be used that will make the earth unlivable. Second, genocide is unethical. These two consider perpetuation of human life at its most basic. We must have a place to inhabit and people to inhabit the place. Genocide is unethical because theories of human group perpetuation require genetic diversity. It is simplistically illustrated by an analogy to trees. The single-variety American chestnut was almost entirely eliminated by one type of infection. Oak trees, with their many varieties, have proved more long lasting. Purposefully shrinking the gene pool by wiping out a specific group, particularly a proved successful group, is thus unethical.

Atrocities and wars between ethnic groups that refuse to see one another as having any common status are still frequent. Atavistic as it may be, war remains a particular threat to groups living in more primitive circumstances where conduct still operates under tribal or other small group conditions. Neighboring groups do not see each other as part of a cohesive larger group or country. Here, each group operates on a physical survival-of-the-fittest basis, where elimination of a rival group is acceptable. Examples are common in Africa and the Middle East. It remains an unanswered question whether groups in these regions can formulate a common goal among their tribal, religious and ethnic factions in order to function as viable countries. Can the small groups forego their "petty tribal loyalties" for a common goal and a much higher likelihood of peace? Perhaps yes. Perhaps no. Yugoslavia is an example of how difficult that can be and that it does not necessarily work out that way.

I believe that war is a less effective means of competition in the current era than it has been in the past. Still, there is no question that, in the foreseeable future, war will continue to be with us and, therefore, the ability to wage war will continue to be needed as a necessary means to "provide for the common defense." This is true for America and for the world as a whole. No reasonable ethical theory can ignore the potential necessity of having to use lethal force for protection. Peace and war represent the opposite ends of the spectrum of the means available to the group. Peace embraces the concept of complete equality and no competition. War represents complete liberty with no rules in force, resulting in maximum competition. War is ethical if it is needed to defend your group from elimination. It is understood that there are those who embrace nonviolence as their personal, subjective ultimate truth. They would pay any price, including their own death, in order to remain nonviolent. The perpetuation theory treats this point of view the same as it does religion or any other personal moral theory. It says that so long as being nonviolent aids the group, it is ethical. If, however, violence is required to preserve the group, then remaining nonviolent is selfish and unethical. Maintaining nonviolence even to the point of personal death does not atone for allowing elimination of the group if elimination could have been prevented by the use of violent means. It is not necessarily the ultimate sacrifice to be willing to die for one's personal "truth." At times, it is more important to be willing to live for one's "truth"—perpetuation. At those times, staying alive and using violence may be needed to preserve the group. It may be the only ethical course. If perpetuation of your group/species is the goal, then not being willing to go to war to defend the group against extermination is de facto unethical.

What about ethics regarding equality of women? Let us first reiterate and clarify how, ethically, equality of opportunity is distinct from equality of value. Equality of opportunity means each member gets an equal chance to compete and demonstrate his or her worth to the group. Equality of value has to do with awarding assets equally regardless of the value or talent they bring to the group. As we have noted, ethically speaking, all members of a group, men and women alike, do not have equal value. However, equality of opportunity for all members of a group is an inherent part of our ethical group formation—part of the deontological obligations and advantages discussed earlier. The group's obligations (remembering the exceptions) are to protect its members, to not interfere with the members' pursuit of happiness, and to assure equal opportunity for all members in order that they may compete so as to enable the group to utilize the best talent. It is appropriate and useful if this competition can result in happiness for the individuals involved, in addition to serving its primary ethical function of aiding the group. The theory of optimum (ethical) group functioning calls for the most capable, most talented group members to assume the most important jobs. They, in each competing generation, are the group leaders. If the group functioning theory is correct, they will give the group the best chance of accomplishing the goal. Simply put, if the group doesn't give women equal opportunity to compete, then the group is unethical because it has eliminated half of its members from the talent search. The group is hopping on one leg rather than walking (or running) on two. Ethically speaking, failure to give women equal opportunity is not so much a disservice to women as individuals as it is that the group cannot afford to waste the talent of half of its members.

There are two more factors to be considered. First, the group must consider protection of its members. Historically, physical strength has been the primary attribute needed for protection. In looking at a timeline of human existence, we quickly see that it is only recently that groups started to develop technologically to the degree that physical strength is less important. Even now, if the world is taken as a whole, physical strength still plays a major role in many (perhaps most) places. In these places women are not well protected if they do not have a strong male defender. In what we call the "first" world, presumably this is no longer the case. (Of course, one wonders whether some of the rural or big city enclaves are in the "first" world.) Presumably, however, in the "first" world that type of protection no longer applies, and physical size no longer restricts equal opportunity for women. We in the "first" world may regard this reliance on physical strength as atavistic adherence to an out-of-date survival-of-the-fittest theory of perpetuation. However, groups must still deal with reality, not idealism. If physical protection for women is still needed then this may well restrict them from equal opportunity. The idealism of thinking it should not be so has no place in ethics. Let me note that choosing this necessary protection, which restricts women's opportunities, is considered the better of unethical choices, not the ethical choice. Groups that have to do this (not to mention those groups that restrict women's opportunities when not forced to do so by physical imperatives) put themselves at a competitive disadvantage versus groups that can derive the optimum benefit from all members—men and women.

The other consideration deals with the bearing and rearing of children. Other than defense and protection from annihilation, there is no job more important to succeeding at perpetuation than creating and rearing the next generation. Only women can bear children. In addition, humans have operated under the cogent theory that women are more talented and capable than men in doing the bulk of the job of raising children, at least through early childhood. This vitally important job is open to competition from men and women, but women have been perceived as more capable and have thus "won" the competition for this position. Of course, much of the "competition" has been dictated by physical attributes. Men, being stronger, could hunt and fight better. Women were needed to nurse the babies. Thus roles developed—and ethically so. Where this situation still prevails in the world today, it continues to be the appropriate ethical choice. To do otherwise would be both foolish and unethical. We cannot abandon *what is* for what we think it *should be*.

There is, however, an ambivalence the first world has in assigning women the primary responsibility, the job, of rearing children. Women are, at least, the intellectual equals of men. (I personally have a suspicion that estrogen could actually give women a statistical IQ advantage.) Other jobs are rewarded more of the assets of the group. Why, then, should women not go where the money is? Why should a woman be more "handicapped" by child rearing responsibilities than a man in competition for jobs outside of the home? In such reasoning, we are forgetting that this job of bearing and raising children is more important than almost any of the other jobs of the group. The only exception is the absolute necessity of defense from threats that could cause elimination of the group. It is an error in ethical thinking that takes child rearing for granted or, worse, takes it as somehow being only a hindrance for women trying to compete for other jobs. The job must be done as well as possible. There is every reason to think that a couple working together to raise children is best. Still, the operative theory would also say that the woman's role is more important, at least in early childhood. While there are monetary losses involved, it is fortunate that there may be no greater source of happiness than seeing this job well done.

Ethics requires that we understand the real world where, in many places, protection for the physically weaker is still needed. Ethics will also recommend that, until a new theory is proven, the group operate as much as possible under the older theory. Thus, women bearing the primary responsibility for child rearing continues to be the ethically recommended theory. In effect, women have been selected as more talented in the competition for this vitally important job. Of course, it is neither required nor needed that all women be involved in doing this particular job. Women not involved in child rearing, (they elected not to have children, they were unable to have children, their children are grown, they had no choice but to work outside the home, etc.) deserve, and ethically are required to have, equal opportunity to compete for any of the other jobs of the group. Their talents are just as valuable as those of the male members of the group. Where physical strength is a determinant for the job to be done, women have to compete with their physical strength. If they are less strong, then that factor will put them at a disadvantage in the competition for that job. Of course, there are fewer and fewer jobs where that is the case. In general, a group's most important jobs have little requirement for physical strength (an exception is some of the jobs in the military) and, ethically speaking, women's talents need to be used where they will provide the greatest benefit to the group.

Restricting equal opportunity for women also violates another prohibition placed on the group—it cannot restrict a member's pursuit of happiness unless that pursuit is detrimental to the group's primary goal. That leads to a specific question regarding pursuit of happiness. If bearing and raising children is a vital job for the group, when is it ethical for a woman, or for that matter a man, to decide for her or his individual happiness not to have children? The answer depends on how many members the group needs in the next generation to accomplish its goal. If more members are not needed, and particularly if more members would be detrimental because of available resources, then it is entirely ethical for women and men to elect to not have children. These women and men then can function ethically in other roles. They compete to demonstrate their talent and do the job they earn. By so doing, they play their part in having the group function smoothly and efficiently trying to accomplish perpetuation. It is an appropriate side benefit if this also brings happiness. However, if the group needs more members, then, ethically speaking, neither women nor men can indulge in their personal preference for happiness at the expense of procreation. Let us note that at this point in history such is not the case.

The frequent enslavement of the Slavic peoples in the first millennium of the Common Era gives us our word for slave, but slavery as a human institution extends into the earliest of times and, in parts of the world, still exists. I do not intend to address whether some combination of circumstances in prehistory or early human history might have made it ethically justifiable to hold slaves rather than kill captives. Slavery has been an integral part of many, perhaps even most, large cultures up until the last perhaps 200 years (Greek, Roman, Islamic, etc.). With the discovery of the Americas, however, large tracts of land came available and slavery developed on a much larger commercial scale as slaves were used to work this land. This volume of traffic dealing with the capture and export of Africans as slaves to the New World represented an order of magnitude not previously encountered. It resulted in a specific unethical situation in America with unethical sequelae that are still extant. It is this specific combination that I will briefly consider.

We are accustomed to dealing with the inappropriateness of slavery as a violation of morals and as an injustice to the individuals enslaved. Ethics, however, looks at the issue from the objective data as to how it affects the group's ability to function in perpetuating itself. The individual suffering involved becomes a secondary issue, related to how that suffering affects the group's goal. The fact that slave owners and traders could morally justify slavery is an example of the subjective, individual, malleable nature of morals and demonstrates why morals cannot be used as a basis for ethics.

Slavery in America was unethical because it resulted from poor theory formation. It indulged the liberty of individual slave owners to do as they pleased in the short term. In so doing, it worked to the detriment of the group by disrupting smooth group functioning and by its lack of long-term reasoning or concerns. The theory formation included data that was objectively erroneous, including the assumption that African slaves were of a different species. The theory also included subjective, interpretative Biblical data (similar data is found in the *Koran/Qur'an*) justifying slavery. Slave owners and traders defended themselves with the oxymoronic concept that freedom and liberty and property rights gave them the right to enslave others. It was a variation on the survival-of-the-fittest theory. Their justification rested on their assumed racial superiority versus those whom they would enslave. It was essentially the same reasoning used by the Greeks 2000 years before. As Russell in *A History of Western Philosophy* notes, since the Greeks were (in their minds) superior to the surrounding races "Plato and Aristotle thought it wrong to make slaves of Greeks, but not of barbarians." (The Romans did not subscribe to this theory and had no problem subsequently enslaving Greeks.)

The slave owners and dealers accrued advantages to themselves without regard to how their actions affected the larger group as a whole. The slave owners were guilty of bringing in a subgroup that did not want to be in the group. The slaves, thus, formed an unnecessary threat to the rest of the group since they represented a constant threat for violent revolt if there was opportunity. The group formation component of the perpetuation theory points out that successful groups work well only if both parties accept each other and if the talents of members are available to benefit the group as a whole. Slaves were de facto part of the group but were not given member status. This is not an ethical part of the theory of group formation and maintenance. Slavery was, from the start, a major source of friction between accepted group members. Virtually any long-term thinking could see no advantage coming to the group as a whole. Even some slave owners, notably Thomas Jefferson, recognized the unethical long-term consequences for America. Nonetheless, Jefferson and the others unethically indulged their own short-term personal advantages to the detriment of group America.

It is worth considering the ethical dilemma of America's founding fathers. Why did they accept slavery in the Constitution that formed the basis for the United States of America? Let's look at it from John Adams' point of view. He and his wife were against slavery. Yet Adams was faced with a Hobson's choice. The slave states in the south would not join if slavery was not accepted. John Adams could accept slavery as part of the Constitution and create America or he could not accept it and forego the founding of the United States of America. He and the other antislavery founders of America accepted what they thought was the better of two unethical choices. It is also noteworthy that 70+ years later Lincoln too thought preservation of America was the more important issue. He would have compromised considerably on the issue of slavery if he could have preserved the Union in so doing. When he found that the only way to preserve the Union was through civil war, then that was the route he accepted. In so doing, he was also able to free the slaves. Before the war started, however, as noted by Jay Winik in his book *April 1865: The Month That Saved America,* in a rebuttal to Horace Greeley, Lincoln wrote, "My paramount object in this struggle is to save the Union and it is not either to save or destroy slavery. If I could save the Union without freeing any slaves, I would do it; and if I could save it by freeing all the slaves I would do it; and if I could save it by freeing some slaves and leaving others alone I would do that." Sometimes the best that can be done is unethical and the better of unethical choices is what must be chosen. Ethics does not have the luxury of dealing with idealism and inaction. Choices in the real world have to be made.

While we can identify the faulty approaches that led to unethical behavior in the institution of slavery, it is in results where ethics is judged. Slavery forced America into a civil war of devastating proportions. The fragmentation of the country and the difficulties of reconstruction were what resulted from the unethical choice of slavery in America. The war was the major, relatively short-term, result that confirmed that slavery was unethical for group-America. The immediate problems that followed the war emphasized that slavery was unethical. The long-term suboptimal (unethical) group functioning caused by slavery and its aftermath is still with us.

Freeing the slaves at the time of the war was a vital step, but it did not correct the deontology problem of improper group formation. Remember the basics. For a smaller group to join the larger, both the larger group and the individuals of the smaller group agree to the obligations that come with the advantages. The new members agree to follow the ethics, or rules, that were objectively developed to accomplish the common goal of the larger group. The larger group (with exceptions implicit when necessary for group survival) is obligated to treat the joining new members as of the same species and therefore to give them equal opportunity to compete. The larger group also guarantees protection of the new members and permits them to pursue happiness. Group-America allowed the slaves to become citizens but failed to live up to its obligations. Protection was flagrantly lacking, as evidenced by lynchings well into the 20th century. Equal opportunity to compete was not given. In addition, education—the cornerstone of future equal opportunity to compete successfully—was not distributed equally. This lack of fulfilling the obligations had serious negative implications on the individuals of the slave-related subgroup regarding their pursuit of happiness. Since many of the advantages of joining group America were not forthcoming, over time, the further unethical spin-off was that the members of this subgroup had little incentive to follow the rules of the larger group and much incentive to look inward to their subgroup for a common goal—to protect the subgroup. When the larger group-America reneged on its part of the bargain, there was little reason for the former slave and slave-descendants to keep their obligations. It is remarkable that, for the most part, these slave-descendant members kept their obligations even while group-America was painfully slow in assuming its obligations.

Group-America continues to deal with the consequences of this earlier, unethical deontological contract. Understanding the ethical problem can, however, lead to theories that can slowly correct the error. The problem has two parties: those individuals who see themselves as descendants from the original slaves, and group-America. At this point, there is incomplete obligation fulfillment on the part of both parties. One party alone cannot make all corrections as deontology and smooth group function require both parties to assume obligations and, thus, both parties need to undergo corrective actions. Over the last 50 years or so, group-America has (finally) taken many appropriate steps. The most basic ones have been assuming the obligations of equal protection and equal opportunity including voting rights and education. In addition, affirmative action is a relatively recent step at corrective action, and it seems to have proved useful. It has been affirmed by the Supreme Court to be used for a finite period. While useful, affirmative action necessarily has some unethical aspects, particularly that it places some less talented members of group-America (Americans of African heritage) ahead of some other Americans who are more talented. This type of suboptimal solution, as has been noted, often must be used in ethics. Ethics must be practical and is forced to deal with the best of the possible solutions, all of which have some unethical components. The least unethical may be the best that can be done. The question for affirmative action now is not whether we should have it, but rather for how long. There will be a point of diminishing returns, and then the unethical results affecting the more talented will no longer be offset by the improvement in the contract between group-America and the descendants of slaves. At that point, ethically speaking, affirmative action will need to cease.

The other half of the deontological contract requires that for all Americans, including members descended from slaves, America must come first. All members have an ethical obligation to group-America to treat all other members honestly, fairly and politely, employing the virtues equally to other group members. Not to do so, to preferentially treat one's subgroup better or to try to benefit one's subgroup to the detriment of America, is just as racist and unethical for blacks as it is for whites. For example, it is just as racist and unethical for an American of African heritage to snub an American of European heritage in Atlanta as it is for the reverse to happen in Boston. Also, all Americans are ethically required to follow the rules/ethics/laws of the country. The high incarceration rate of Americans of the slave-descendant subgroup may yet reflect some racism on the part of group-America, but there is little doubt that it also reflects the fact that most of those incarcerated feel little obligation to follow the rules of group-America. Since group-America had the initial ethical deontological failing that led to the current problem, it is appropriate that group-America first correct its deficiencies. However, the problem cannot be corrected until Americans of the slave-descendant subgroup also assume their obligations. Both parties must fulfill their obligations in order for the advantages of group formation to outweigh the disadvantages. Only in this manner can the deontological quid pro quo properly function.

Education is the key to all ethical behavior. It is also the key that permits each party in the deontological contract to fulfill its obligations and to receive its advantages. If the younger Americans of the slave-descendant subgroup are underemphasizing education because it is a "white man's" game, then this needs to be recognized as self-defeating behavior and corrected. The talents of members who shun education will never be able to be fully realized and that is detrimental to group-America as well as to the uneducated individual. Marginalizing education severely limits performance in America's competition for talent. America will suffer because all available talent is not developed and utilized. The affected individuals will suffer since, by doing poorly in the group's competition, they will receive a smaller share of America's assets—they will make less money than those with education. Just as denying equal education to Americans of the slave-descendant subgroup was egregiously unethical on the part of group-America initially, it is ironically unethical for these Americans to not take advantage of education when it is offered.

It is necessary for both parties to move forward on the road to ethical behavior and cohesive group functioning because it is clearly in the best interests of both parties. Group-America will benefit in its pursuit of the group goal of perpetuation and the slave-descendants will benefit in the pursuit of the individual goal of happiness. As time goes on it will get harder to correct this ethical problem because increases in other subgroup populations will decrease the percentage of Americans with interest or concerns regarding American slavery or the Civil War. In addition, racial heritage is increasingly fuzzy. The October 2003 *Scientific American* reported that approximately 70 percent of Americans who consider themselves Black have some Caucasian heritage and 20 percent of Americans who consider themselves Caucasian have some Black heritage. Add to this the increasing numbers of Americans of Asian and Hispanic heritage and the intermixing of all racial groups of Americans. America is, indeed, a mixed breed and this is one of its biggest strengths. New members of group America, native born and immigrants, are looking to the future, competing to do well, and pursuing happiness within the governmental/political/ethical structure that America has. Group-America has an ethical Constitutional obligation to live up to its half of the contract regarding protection and equal opportunity. It may require further work to completely fulfill these obligations to those who consider themselves in the subgroup of slave-descendants. Still those regarding themselves as slave-descendants, like all Americans of any racial heritage, must give up "their petty tribal loyalties" and, in order to be ethical, place America first.

In addition to its unethical effects on group-America (not to mention the unethical effects on Africa), slavery in America was tragic and devastating for millions of individuals. In our section on esthetics we recognized that lack of happiness (tragedy and suffering inflicted on individuals) contributes significantly to poor group functioning and can be a major factor in the unethical results. Such was the case with slavery. The personal tragedies are not to be forgotten. Still, it was the difficulties for the group with the Civil War and the racial discord produced that made slavery unethical. The long-term results from slavery kept and continue to keep America from smooth group functioning and from using all of its members' talents to best advantage. While this view may lack sentiment and may seem inadequate in view of the personal tragedies, it is the objective basis for the American experience with slavery being unethical. Suboptimal group functioning can lead the group to fail in its goal of perpetuation or, because of the inefficiencies, lead to its being less competitive and replaced by another more efficient country as the leader of the world group. If that were to happen (or perhaps when it inevitably will happen) it is quite likely that there will be less happiness (prosperity and advantage) for all members of group-America.

What are the ethics of suicide? The first thing suicide suffers from is the fact that in the English language it seems to be the only word available to deal with several kinds of self-termination. I will discuss the ethics of suicide as it applies to four situations. The first is clinical depression not otherwise related to end-of-life or other physical problems. The second is end-of-life suicide. The third is suicide for the protection of the group. The fourth is ritual, culturally sanctioned suicide.

Suicide relating to depression is unethical. It is a selfish move done to satisfy an individual's desires. Only when the suicide is done for reasons that would not impair the group can it be ethical. Not being able to "face life" is not an ethical justification. An individual's first obligation is to first consider how it affects the larger group—that is, how the suicide would affect family, friends or fellow workers. To do otherwise impairs the group's ability and is thus unethical. Only after that obligation has been addressed can the individual's desire for happiness be pursued. (In this case the happiness is relief from suffering—improvement in the negative side of happiness.) Suffering, whether psychological or physical, is primarily the individual's problem. Thus, it is the individual's job/obligation to endure the suffering *if* so doing is beneficial to the group's functioning and attainment of the group goal. We identify depression as an illness, presumably out of the control of the afflicted individual, and so this judgment seems harsh. Identifying depression as an illness and developing treatment can be ethical because it may help to avoid the unethical consequences of suicide. If treatment is available and not used, this may constitute an unethical inaction on the part of the group as well as on the part of the individual. Nonetheless, ethics is judged objectively on the results not on intent. Justice (we will remember that justice is a moral problem but an ethical tool) will let us use intent to judge depression-related suicide. Justice would have us understand why it happened and why we might excuse it. This approach is most likely beneficial to friends and family members harmed by the suicide. Still, depression-related suicide that negatively impacts family, friends and group functioning would be considered unethical based on objective results. The individual's desires ethically come second to the group's needs even in regard to suicide.

Depression-related suicide may be considered ethical if the person is such an unrecoverable drain on the group that his or her demise benefits the group. Admittedly, a deeply depressed person is not in position to make that judgment, but this is another of those uncomfortable discoveries that comes from having an objective goal. It is the result that counts. If the suicide benefits the group in pursuing its goal, then it is considered ethical.

End-of-life issues raise another question. Second in importance only to doing what is best for the group is the individual's right to pursue happiness. As we remember, individual pursuit of happiness is permitted unless it impairs the ability of the group to accomplish the primary goal. When an objective situation is reached where an individual no longer has the ability to have happiness and, in addition, can no longer assist the larger group, it is not unethical to terminate oneself. Happiness is a spectrum with euphoria at one end and extreme suffering at the other. Relief of suffering is an identifiable form of the pursuit of happiness. At the end of life, suicide by an individual who is suffering and no longer capable of receiving happiness is not unethical if such self-termination does not impair the ability of the group. In this case, the group should not keep the person from seeking whatever relief or happiness he or she desires. In this situation, if the group restricts the individual from this pursuit of happiness, then the group is acting unethically.

Suicide for the good of the group is potentially ethical. This is seen most vividly in military conflicts when a person or a small contingent is left behind to permit the retreat of the larger unit. It is also seen in the kamikaze dive bombings by the Japanese in WWII. The suicide bombings used by the Palestinians today may or may not be ethical. Whether or not these bombings are actually accomplishing anything good (i.e., truly ethical) for the Palestinians is the important question. That involves examining the data and the resultant theory that has led to the bombings, along with examining the results and consequences. The key to deciding whether these bombings are ethical is whether or not the theory supporting the suicide bombings is correct. It could be helping the Palestinians or it could be that objective data are not being used and that a combination of motives for revenge and personal, religious confirmation is forcing a bad theory onto the Palestinians. In Israel/Palestine we have an open philosophical conflict between the Israelis whose survival (the primary goal) is threatened and the Palestinians whose lives have been made so miserable that they cannot achieve happiness (the goal secondary only to survival). For Palestinians, existence has little happiness. Their group theory says a suicide, with additional Israeli casualties, will help the group. In this case, there are no group ethical barriers to such action. Survival is obviously primary to Israel. However, until they find a way to enable the Palestinians to achieve happiness within Israel's framework of survival, there will be no termination of the conflict. In the present situation, the Palestinians have only slightly less to lose than the Israelis.

There is one other ethical suicide practice. This is a ritual suicide that is sanctioned, essentially presanctioned, by the culture. This type of self-termination is seen more in association with eastern rather than western traditions. It can be suicide sanctioned as atonement for family, group or personal failures, or it could be an end-of-life issue even if the person or persons are not immediately terminally ill. Such deaths are not unethical if they do not negatively impact other members of the group or the death is for the good of the group.

What about the death penalty? The death penalty is a means that can serve as an example of justice in general. In a system that functions perfectly there is no problem with the death penalty. The members of the group that have gone that far beyond the accepted rules are no longer helping the group. Eliminating them serves the group well. What about the imperfect application of the death penalty—putting to death an innocent person? Are there enough resources to guard against mistakes? Are there enough resources that it is not necessary for the group to kill the presumed offenders?

In considering justice and the death penalty, it must be understood that the only way to be completely effective in guarding against punishing an innocent person is to never punish anybody. Inevitably, some people unjustly accused will be punished. Still, justice and punishment are tools that are used for the benefit of the larger group. It is like the war situation where foot soldiers are charging an entrenched enemy and the artillery is bombarding the enemy. If the artillery stops the bombardment too soon, the enemies will pop up out of their foxholes and kill more of your soldiers. Here, the bombardment must continue until your own advanced men start to fall from your own artillery bombardment. This achieves the goal of taking the enemy position and does so with the fewest casualties. So it is done with "justice." It is not perfect. It is a means not an end in itself, and justice must be administered in keeping with the larger group's goal of achieving the primary objective. The fewer that are punished "unjustly" the better. Some innocents will, however, pay a price. That is what is required for the larger group to have the best chance of achieving its goal. With specific regard to the death penalty, if the group has the available resources I suggest it would be less unethical, and more just, to do away with the death penalty and substitute life imprisonment in order to avoid the death of the occasional innocent. Today, in the United States it might also be more economical to keep them imprisoned until they die. In some countries and circumstances, however, this is not an affordable solution because they do not have the resources to afford life in prison for those convicted. The decision for the group will be based on these considerations: whether killing the convicted helps group functioning, whether it does more harm than good for the group and whether there are sufficient resources to imprison them and not kill them.

What are the ethics of population control including birth control and abortion? As with all issues it starts by looking at what is best for the group as a whole, remembering that all actions are means and can be ethical or unethical depending on the time and circumstances. In the past, there has been a need for high birth rates to counter threats including high infant mortality, infectious diseases including plagues, poor understanding of sanitation, and the need for workers and fighters. A high birth rate has been a successful method by which groups, less successful in the relatively short term of war's competition, have had better long-term success—a very useful intergroup competition strategy. When important for group survival, avoiding reproduction for individual reasons of happiness is unethical.

Today, there are fewer and fewer places where unlimited breeding and reproduction can still be objectively justified as being in the best interests of any larger secular group. There are many countries where it is clearly detrimental to keep birth rates high. In those countries, being unwilling to use birth control and abortion is unethical. China, for example, is ethical in its efforts to decrease its overall birth rate. Iran has come to the same conclusion. The United States is still working with older theories and has not started actively working against population increase. It is a safe prediction that the arguments being used today to justify not using birth control will be (within the next 50 or so years) viewed very similar to arguments about how many angels can stand on the head of a pin. That is to say, completely irrelevant. Likewise, when there is no advantage to the goal of the country, not letting people decide what is in their best interest in their pursuit of happiness—whether or not to have an abortion—is unethical. Remember that second only to what is needed for group perpetuation is the need for people to be able to pursue their own happiness. For the larger group, the country, to limit the individual members' pursuit of happiness, when such pursuit does not affect the country's needs, is unethical. Regarding pregnancy, one could argue that protection of members of the group requires that the group protect the fetus. The stronger counter argument is that the fetus is not a member until he or she joins and he or she cannot join until born. The same is true for naturalized citizens. Until they actually sign on the dotted line, they are not members of the group. That moment must actually happen. For example, many non-American pregnant women pass through America and their children never become American citizens because they deliver elsewhere. If they happen to be born in America, only then can they claim citizenship. If you are not yet a member of the group, then you do not have the group's protection afforded you. Full members of the group, in this case women who are pregnant, have full protection, and these women also have the right to pursue their own happiness unless it negatively impacts on the group's ability to achieve its primary goal. Hence, in these times, ethically speaking, the country has no business or justification for interfering in the decisions of its women members regarding birth control and abortion.

A related ethical problem has to do with how much of a group's resources can be expended sustaining the frail and incapable members. This problem involves any and all elements of the group's population ranging from demented older persons to the very low birth weight premature infants, to the severely handicapped and other unemployable noncontributors. We examined this problem earlier in understanding the ethics (as opposed to the morals) of Eskimo infanticide. The problem of the death penalty is also similar. The answer lies in the group's available resources. In a wealthy country, the group can afford to expend resources to sustain these noncontributors. If the group's needs are such that it cannot afford to support a noncontributing segment, then, ethically speaking, it need not, in fact must not, sustain them. That was the point made earlier in the ethical (as opposed to moral) justification for Eskimo infanticide. If keeping noncontributors alive uses resources the main group requires to accomplish the primary goal, then you let some or even all of them go, just as must be done in an overloaded lifeboat. In the third world, many noncontributors cannot be saved. The connection is easier to see in the example of Eskimo infanticide but all groups and countries have the same problem. Technology has imposed on the first world the ability to keep the very premature and the decrepit alive much longer, even if there is no reasonable hope that they can ever or ever again be mentally active and contributors to the group. Pouring unlimited resources into this segment of a group's population is very difficult (I would say impossible) to ethically justify. Such action diverts funds from contributing members and diverts funds from other threat solutions (long-term threats are always particularly vulnerable to underfunding). It would inevitably compromise the group's best chance of accomplishing its goal. The decisions are difficult and also involve who (if anyone) is receiving happiness from sustaining these members. Still, no group is exempt from having to make these decisions if they are to succeed in perpetuation.

What about ethics regarding the environment? First, just as it is true that war may be necessary and ethical, so it is true that environmentalism is necessary and ethical. It is the lifeboat problem writ large. Again, it is a balancing problem. The balance this time is between the current generation in this moment in time versus future generations and future needs. The fact that an individual or individual subgroup "owns" a given piece of property does not give them the absolute liberty to do anything they like to it. No one lives but one lifetime and so all ownership of property is temporary. Multiple generations of humans will need and "own" that same property. Ownership of a seat on lifeboat earth does not grant people permission to knock a hole in their part of the boat. Current owners can use the property to the extent their use will not impair the ability of the future group to accomplish the primary goal. (This particular environmental discussion involves primary ethical rules; it does not consider esthetic considerations involving being "good neighbors" and secondary ethical rules.) This restraint has both immediate and long-term aspects that must be taken into consideration. Short-term use or abuse of property, in this case for a generation or a few generations, cannot be permitted to compromise group perpetuation. It would be unethical. Taken to the extreme, this is why the concept of Mutually Assured Destruction is ipso facto unethical. (As noted earlier, however, the use of smaller nuclear arms is not necessarily unethical.) Currently, we have just one useable planet for humanity and it will need to last for more than a few decades. Proper attention to the environment is ethical and an absolutely necessary, conservative position to assume. The concept of perpetuation must deal with more than the current generation.

Using up resources, more than can be renewed, puts a burden on succeeding generations. It does not matter that resources have always been used in this way. The fact that someone's father and grandfather cut trees for a living does not mean that future generations will necessarily be able to cut trees for a living. The same goes for such activities as fishing, hunting, mining, farming, etc. It also doesn't matter if the individual and subgroup involved is from the first world or third world, Nomadic tribe, Inuit or Indian. Ethics deals with results and not with intent or tradition. Consideration for subsequent generations is always a necessity. This becomes a real conundrum when you consider some of today's third world groups and some, still extant, subsistence groups. Their resources are vanishing. If they don't use them they cease to exist, and if they do use them the next generation may not exist. Yet, if the current generation ceases to exist, they know the next generation won't be here. So, the subgroup feels ethically justified in using the resources as they have in the past. What this really represents is a failure of their ethical system to account for long-term threats and a failure to adjust to changing times. They should have adjusted their conduct sooner so as to avoid this problem and give themselves the best chances for survival. Their circumstances required change and they did not adjust as needed. Ethics does not accept excuses or finger pointing. You accomplished the goal or you didn't, and it doesn't matter if it was somebody else's fault. It will be interesting to see if the first world, the current world leaders, can adjust population and environmental resource use so as to avoid, in the future, the kind of dilemma faced today by parts of the third world, Nomadic tribes and subsistence groups.

In our liberty–equality spectrum we can see why the proponents of more liberty with fewer rules (in America, the Republicans of the moment) can more readily accept war and less readily accept environmentalism, while the reverse is true of the equality end of the spectrum with more rules (the Democrats of the moment). War is maximum competition (recall that the hallmark of liberty is competition) with no rules in force. That situation is anathema to the equality end of the spectrum. On the other hand, protecting the environment restricts the liberty of a current generation in their use of the property they own. As we discussed, ownership of a portion of earth for one lifetime does not grant permission to misuse it so as to jeopardize the ability of subsequent generations to sustain themselves. Ethically speaking, property owners do not have complete liberty to do as they will to their property. Some rules are needed to restrict property rights to ensure long-term survival and equality for future generations. Both positions—war and environmentalism—can be and are, in the proper situations, ethical. They furnish examples of why neither end of the spectrum can function ethically for the long term without considering the other end.

Now, let us consider one of the problems of competition as it relates to the environment. Global warming has gathered enough data to be generally accepted as a very likely correct theory. How do we change our conduct to give ourselves the best chance to counter this threat? Carbon dioxide emissions are proposed as a significant contributor to the problem. The United States is the major contributor to carbon dioxide emissions. The cause and effect theories regarding global warming are imperfect but the part about contributions from carbon dioxide is, more than a little, credible. The United States has, at the moment, competitively assumed the "alpha dog" role among the world countries. Other countries, less successful in the current competition, will try to use this issue to handicap the United States in its energy use and give their group some advantage. The United States will be very reluctant to change conduct since this conduct gave it the edge in competition. The best way to address this problem is with epistemology and logic, with objective data and objective theories. In fact, nowhere is the need for correct data and the best possible processing into theories better seen than in this example. If the theory for the role of carbon dioxide emissions in global warming holds up, then it is categorically unethical for the United States to continue to go its own way. The United States is definitely part of the larger community of nations. As such, it cannot indulge in its own short-term happiness or gratification to the long-term detriment of not only itself, but of the world community. My opinion is that even if global warming is not a perfect theory (remember that no objective theory ever is) it is a reasonable theory based on objective data. Thus, it represents a long-term threat big enough to require action be taken now. If later the theory is improved and does not include carbon dioxide emissions as a significant cause, then it would not be hard to reverse back to the original course. However, it would most likely be very hard, perhaps impossible, to rectify the situation if we go too far on the current course. Call it insurance. Such insurance would help cover an eventuality that we hope won't happen but, ethically speaking, we should choose to pay this short-term price because we cannot afford to ignore the long-term threat. Ignoring threats is unethical.

Developing worldwide threats to the environment calls into focus the ethical necessity to develop a more coherent single-world group. This will be necessary to deal with the environmental problems of population, pollution and diminishing resources that affect and involve the world as a whole. Worldwide pooling of talents and resources is also the approach that gives humans the best chance to expand off earth, which will be key to increasing our long-term possibilities of survival. The feasibility of colonizing Mars has been outlined in scientific journals, and to inhabit Mars would improve chances of perpetuation both by increasing our resources and by environmental diversification. Our ethical job is to give humans the best chance of perpetuation. We can't depend on just one planet if we have other options. We must expand our concept of environmentalism. It would be a huge advantage, a very big insurance policy, to not be dependent on just one planet for perpetuation (remember asteroid impacts and the dinosaurs). I predict that we will stick with old habits and that too many of us will be slow to believe the need for population control worldwide. Then, the need for colonies off earth will be demanding. If it can be done, and we already theorize that it can, we will have to try. The concept of environment is much bigger than we have traditionally considered it to be. Research and development in space exploration and understanding are not just academic intellectual exercises. They are critical for long-term planning and necessary ethical things to do.

I never said the process of deciding how to adjust our ethical systems would be easy. It is uncomfortable to recognize that not supporting the least talented may be ethical, that war may be ethical, that the virtues are not always ethical, that essentially all means might be expressed as having a greater or lesser probability of being ethical. We yearn for fixed "truths" that an ever-changing natural world does not have. We thus seek our own subjective, often supernatural, "truths." These are "truths" for each of us as individuals but cannot apply objectively to the human group as a whole.

I have outlined the problem and the organizational structure of philosophy. This organization and structure lead us through the process of determining human conduct, determining how we should live, if we as a species are to perpetuate ourselves. The most difficult obstacle to overcome is to accept the fact that our individual "truths," our own morals and our individual pursuit of happiness must always be secondary to the group's goal. We must accept that conduct for the group's goal must be dictated by objective, group acceptable theories. It is these objective theories that define ethical, not our individual "truths." It is wise to realize the most important thing in life, perpetuating the species, can also be the very same thing that brings the individual happiness. We can and should derive pleasure from helping the group function smoothly, nurturing the next generation, teaching lessons learned so mistakes are not repeated, developing theories to unite the world to become a single functioning group, researching and acquiring data and developing theories regarding our world and universe, and other conduct that promotes the group's ability to achieve its primary goal of perpetuation. Happy is the man or woman who likes the job and goal he or she must work toward. We should let ethical conduct bring us pleasure because the group requires that we act ethically, regardless of our inclinations.

If united, we humans have a chance of continuing for a while, perhaps not as long or as successfully as the dinosaurs, but still longer than we can as a divided planet. One cannot help but laugh at our notion that dinosaurs failed as a species. Indeed, we have not yet survived one percent of the time of the dinosaurs. United we can counter threats much more efficiently than if divided. My opinion is that we had better get united sooner rather than later.

My chief worry is about the divisiveness created by our multiple religions and subjective faiths. I fear Lucretius was right, *"Tantum religio portuit suadere malorum."* I fear the evil to which religion can push us. Religions often purport to hold the key to an afterlife that follows death. This faith in a particular religion is critically important to many people, providing the happiness needed to get the secular job done. Yet, there is danger in looking to religion and afterlife for all answers. Some religious people can justify eliminating secular life for all of us in order to attain their religious goal. Life is more important than the meaning of life. Without life there is no meaning of life. Religion must be accepted as the second place to look for ethical values. The primary, objective, secular goal takes precedence and that goal is the primary determinant of ethics. This proper sequence is far too important to humanity for us to get it wrong.

I didn't start out to formulate an ethical theory. But there it is—the functional organization and structure of philosophy unavoidably provides an ethical theory. Could my basic assumption be wrong? Is there another human function more important than perpetuating the species? I don't think so. I think prioritizing perpetuation of the human species fits Bertrand Russell's definition of "objective truth" quoted at the start of the section on The Starting Assumption. Still, we need to come back to this question because, as I said at the start, if you don't agree with the starting point, then you can ignore the results. Each generation will create objective results—consequences that will result from each generation's actions. The consequences might be a devastated earth or an overpopulated earth. We can pretend there is no future beyond our current generation. We can make the earth free of humans and full of other animals. We can stay divided and compete to make our "one true religion" dominant. There are almost unlimited possibilities within the "realm of ends." My starting assumption was, and still is, that the most important of the possibilities is human survival, perpetuation of our species. If we assign top priority to perpetuation then we understand that we will adjust our conduct to maximize our chances of accomplishing this particular end. This conduct is our ethics. Ethics is the functional final product of philosophy. Ethics is the means by which we hope to accomplish our goal. Does the end justify the means? If survival of the species is our most important, desired end then it better. We certainly don't want the means dictating one of the less important other ends to us. The concept that ethics must be constantly adjusted bothers many of us, but that's the way it works out. We hope to ensure perpetuation of the human species—the greatest good and the most important end—and for that purpose we adjust our ethics—our means.

POSTSCRIPT

"What's it all about, Alfie
Is it just for the moment we live
...
And if life belongs only to the strong, Alfie,
What will you lend on an old golden rule?"
—Hal David–Burt Bacharach

Answers - $1.00
Correct Answers - $2.00
Opinions - $.50
Dumb looks are still free
—Barbershop Philosophy

This book specifically addresses the Karl Popper comments quoted in the introduction. These can be paraphrased as "What important problem has philosophy posed?" and "What is the organized structure of philosophy that can deal with this problem?" The problem for philosophy comes from understanding the fundamental function of human beings. How must we conduct ourselves in order to give humanity the best chance of continuing to perpetuate the human species? Philosophy is the structure we have designed to address this problem. It consists of the human group acquiring data, using the data to develop cause and effect theories, and using the theories to advise the group of the conduct most likely to enable group survival. The "carrots" that reward our individual efforts in accomplishing this group goal are individual happiness and satisfaction. Understanding these interrelated functions of theory development, ideal conduct for the group, and individual happiness reveals the necessary structure, organization and prioritization for our lives.

In the opening paragraph of the introduction I said there were three questions that started me on this trip. Using the functional structure described in this writing I have found my answers to those questions. First, if there is only a single person existing can he or she do anything unethical? No, I have found he or she cannot. Ethics is a group problem not an individual problem. He or she can do things that are immoral but not unethical.

Second, how can we reconcile the differing philosophies of Nietzsche and Christ? This is the same question posed to Alfie in the song quoted at the start of this postscript. The answer is that we cannot function with either complete unadulterated love and the golden rule or unfettered strength. Christ and Nietzsche represent the extremes of a continuum on the balance board of liberty and equality. Nietzsche represents the far end of individual liberty with the importance of strength and competition and Christ represents the far end of equality with the equal value of individuals. Neither philosophical approach can work without incorporating some elements of the other. The balance, if correct (ethical), will permit the group to accomplish its goal of perpetuation of the species. The reconciliation comes in recognizing that each must accept some parts of the other's approach in order to achieve the goal.

Third, how do we know the Holocaust was wrong if we don't have religion (from the radio-evangelist point of view, specifically Christianity and the *Bible*) to guide us? There are two questions here. The answer to the first is that religion is entirely subjective. It can be used by individuals to rationalize anything. It may be most religious adherents, including Christians, are nice people who believe religion teaches them the Holocaust was wrong. Yet, religion has, as we all know, often been used to justify killing others. In fact, throughout history, the Jews have perhaps suffered more killing justified by religion, particularly Christianity, than has any other group. Christianity's historic role in persecution of the Jews makes it an irony for a Christian evangelist to use Christianity and the *Bible* to say that the Holocaust was wrong. One might say that it requires more than a little "chutzpah." Christianity, as many other religions, can be used either to justify the Holocaust or to damn it. It has no objective standard by which to measure the Holocaust.

The objective, nonreligious answer to the question comes from our developed understanding of group formation, efficient smoothly working groups and maintaining genetic diversity among humans. Germany was a working group; Jews were accepted members of this working group. The Jews were obligated to follow the rules of group-Germany, which they did, including going to war when the group demanded it in World War I. They were successful in the intragroup competition and displayed considerable talent in aiding the group. Other less successful and likely less talented (Christian) members then tried to eliminate the competition—the Jews. This was detrimental to the larger group (some of their most talented members were no longer able to help the group) and murderously detrimental to selected individual members of the group—the Jews. These actions were a gross violation of the deontological contract and were unethical. The actions violated the group obligation of protection for its members and violated the obligation of equal opportunity for its members. For group-Germany, this combination of obligation failures seriously compromised both the short-term and the long-term ability of Germany to perpetuate its group. Finally, trying to annihilate a particularly successful genetic group of humans is unethical in the context of world humanity. Genetic diversity is a basic ingredient, a fundamental requirement for producing talent that the world needs. Jews had proven talented and were clearly valuable. Their value, in the long term, is not restricted to one country group. The world group has need for and claim on all human genetic material. It is needed to produce the varieties of talents needed. It is needed to counter unknown diseases. To try to eliminate such a genetic asset was not only unethical for group-Germany but also unethical on a world scale—a crime against humanity.

As well, the Holocaust represented millions of individual tragedies. Almost all (remember there will always be exceptions to subjective individual moral concepts—the Nazis themselves serving as an example in this case) concepts of justice based on individual moral values would condemn it as wrong. Ethics, however, is about the group's goal. Individuals are relevant primarily in how they fit into the group plan to achieve the group goal. There are no grades of more or less ethical but there are grades of unethical. On the scale of 1 to 100 the highest numbers are what we would label evil. I arbitrarily use the scale of more than 90 as evil. It severely impairs group functioning. The concept of nuclear MAD is, for example, inherently evil and would score 100 on the scale since it would completely eliminate human existence. Anything that did not eliminate humans would score less than 100 but those more than 90 would still qualify as evil on my scorecard. In objectively assessing how unethical the Holocaust was we first look at the damage it did to group-Germany. It was part of the aggression and war that devastated the country. It was part of the war that caused Germany to be divided and has diminished Germany's ability to function optimally as a group for 59 years (and still counting). Even after being reunited, the half of Germany that was subjected to a failed experiment in equality (communism) still does not function as a fully contributing part of the whole. The Holocaust eliminated a large number of talented members of group-Germany, the Jews, who, with their descendants, would have helped improve the functioning of the group. The long-term effects of the Holocaust will continue to impair German functioning for at least 100 years. It will take that long for East Germany to be fully reintegrated into group-Germany. Germany's valuable Jewish constituency will most likely never be recovered.

On a world scale, Jews came to believe they could no longer depend on the deontological contract with its obligation of protection by the larger group. The Holocaust provided the necessary catalyst for other members of the world group to give the Jews a homeland, which was carved out of territory already claimed by another group. The Holocaust was, thus, a significant factor that has resulted in the Middle East crisis. The creation of Israel has formed the basis for conflict and violent disruption between the two groups claiming the land. It has negatively affected the functioning of both the local subgroups—the Arabs and the Jews. The world group has, also, been forced to be involved. The acrimonious relationship between the Arabs and the Jews, fallout in significant part precipitated by the Holocaust, has become a significant obstacle keeping the world from making more progress towards the formation of a single-world group. This situation, this fallout, has seriously impaired the world's ability to focus on other worldwide threats held in common and has impaired its ability to fully consider other long-term threats to humanity. It has, thereby, negatively impacted world group function and decreased our ability to deal with perpetuation. Thus, the Holocaust objectively rates well over 90 out of 100 on the scale of unethical. That is the definition of evil. No additional, subjective religious condemnation is needed.

My writing represents an outsider's look at philosophy, based on what it does rather than what it is. It is not an in-depth look at any one aspect of philosophy, and my interests have run a mile wide and an inch deep. As a "left brain" outsider, I have looked for, and not found, a coherent structure of philosophy. This writing represents what I developed that works for me. This approach gives me a structure and a frame of reference that help me make sense of problems I see in the world today. It helps me understand that some actions I abhor can, indeed, be seen as potentially ethical. The suicide bombings in the Middle East are the prime example. As noted earlier, the groups promoting suicide are ethically obligated to review the objective data and theories to judge whether these bombings are, in fact, ethical and help the group to survive or whether they, instead, gratify some individuals' personal religious concepts of happiness and do not help the group. That, of course, is the problem with having an objective basis for deciding ethical versus unethical—no person can assume his or her subjective moral judgments are necessarily ethically correct. It's the philosophical equivalent of the old adage in fishing that "all fishermen are liars except you and me—and sometimes I wonder about you." In philosophy, just as in fishing, an objective scale and ruler are required to show what is correct and ethical.

For me, and others, history is a good starting point from which to approach philosophy. (Indeed, Russell's *A History of Western Philosophy* contains perhaps as much history as it does philosophy.)

History forces one to consider how philosophy works in reality. The works of Will and Ariel Durant, particularly *The Story of Civilization,* gave an invaluable flow and continuity to history. For me, reading this work was the equivalent of a second college education. Different perspectives on history can also be helpful. For example, Howard Zinn's *A People's History of the United States* and Paul Johnson's *A History of the American People* gave me food for thought on equality versus liberty, and Jacques Barzun's *From Dawn to Decadence,* with yet another approach to history, led me to consider and define decadence. I found reading about the world's multiple religions fascinating in its own right, but particularly so when integrated into history. Religion's large role in history, and in people's lives in general, makes appreciating where religion should fit into philosophy and life critical. The functional structure of philosophy leads us to understand the necessity of the separation of ethics and morals—state and church.

I believe all persons going into a field that involves intergroup relationships, particularly politics, should read both *The Analects of Confucius* and Machiavelli's *The Prince* and *Discourses.* It's interesting that the West assigns such a pejorative connotation to the term "Machiavellian." (There's nothing like a realist to spoil the theoretical party.) We symbolically kill the messenger because Machiavelli's pragmatic (and ethical) approach conflicts with the academic ivory tower of morals and idealism. Consider this quote. "As bad promises are better broken than kept, I shall treat this as a bad promise, and break it, whenever I shall be convinced that keeping it is adverse to the public interest." This mirrors Machiavelli's perhaps most maligned quote, " . . . a wise prince cannot and should not keep his pledge when it is against his interest to do so and when his reasons for making the pledge are no longer operative." The first quote, however, is from our venerated, practical, ethical president, Abraham Lincoln, just three days before he was assassinated. (See Jay Winik's *April 1865: The Month That Saved America* and Carl Sandburg's *Abraham Lincoln The War Years, 1864-1865.*) Pragmatism is a necessary trait of ethics because it involves managing priorities. Because priorities must be maintained, often the least unethical approach is the best that can be done.

Philosophy is based on epistemology and logic. It comes back to Confucius' admonition to act from knowledge and "pick the best (information)" available. The key to appropriate reasoning and being able to pick the best information is education. It is the foundation that enables the process of reason to unlock the theories we need for describing ethical conduct. It is the critical process whereby we avoid past ethical mistakes, understand problems and develop the best possible solutions to current and future threats. It is also the key that all members must have for the equal opportunity competition used to show ability and value to the group. It is the key that enables the group and its members to distinguish between the truly talented leaders and the demagogues, for only with education, and a firm understanding of the goal, can group members separate the unethical, selfish pandering of the demagogue from the ethical, but sometimes hard, choices made by talented leaders such as Lincoln. It is education that enables us to separate subjective from objective. If philosophy can be said to embrace one vital core value in its search for ethics, this core is education.

I have dabbled lightly in some of the works of classical philosophy and read more deeply in others. In my research, I was looking to see how particular points of view fit into the whole. My tendency was to look for the type of approach used by a particular writer and to find the basis of his or her argument. Particularly with those using subjective bases, I was less interested to see all the details they developed after that point. This may well mean I missed obvious and important meanings of some writers. No doubt, I neglected major philosophic contributors including, perhaps, writers who, like me, also prefer an objective basis for philosophy. Regardless, it has been an interesting trip. I came to know many writers with whom I would enjoy dinner and conversation over a bottle of wine. (I find it an interesting game to decide whom, from throughout history, you might invite to an eight-person dinner party similar to what Steve Allen did on an old television show.)

I have tried to give specific credit where I included ideas or concepts used by various writers. There are few notes or specific references because this is not a research paper. This book is about a set of ideas built on the objective goal of perpetuation of the species and including the idea that liberty and equality are reciprocal values. Building on those two concepts (over nine years) resulted in the structure and organization described in this writing. I first read the concept of the reciprocal relationship of liberty and equality in the Durants' works. It is found in Vol. 11 of *The Story of Civilization—The Age of Napoleon,* pages 153-154. Perpetuation of the species did not specifically come from another writer. I consider it to be a basic tenet of biology. I will, however, note two other references that also use man's animal nature as of primary importance in developing ethical behavior. In *Natural Goodness,* Philippa Foot approaches behavior from a natural point of view and likens "the basis of moral evaluation to that of the evaluation of behaviour in animals." A century earlier Herbert Spencer (who originated the term "survival of the fittest"), in his *Principals of Ethics,* dealt extensively with conduct directly related to natural existence. This work posited that, along with physical evolution, man's conduct is also evolving (Darwin's evolutionary concepts were at the forefront), and man's "moral principals must conform to physical necessities." Though I never saw the exact phrase in Spencer, I assume it was he whom Nietzsche criticized in *The Gay Science* as having "erroneous moral doctrine . . . One holds that what is called good preserves the species, while what is called evil harms the species."

Shinto particularly, and perhaps other eastern philosophies, better appreciates the primary importance of the group as opposed to the individual. This being the case, I would expect that in-depth knowledge of this philosophy and culture could be fruitful reading on the group-preservation-first approach. I think it very likely that the Western reverence for the individual has forced the inductive reasoning process into Western philosophy. To a very real extent the individual represents the particular while the group represents the general. If one's prejudices and philosophic traditions support the primacy of the individual (overtly from Descartes *cogito*—*I* think therefore *I* am but, even before, more subtly, in that philosophy was largely funneled through religion, which, as we have seen, is inherently an individual pursuit) then one is unwittingly forced into suboptimal, inductive reasoning by this assumed starting point—*i.e.,* arguing from the individual/particular to the group/general.

I have assumed that there is no better reference on theory formation than Karl Popper's *The Logic of Scientific Discovery*. His concept of falsifiability is invaluable in determining objectivity. As an aside, I find there is a strong tendency among philosophers to "do as I say do, not as I do." Popper has told us (and it is fair to say philosophy is in, at least, theoretical agreement) how theories are built based on solid data. To be useful for the group, theories need to be able to be testable and, if falsified, changed. Somehow the various theories of ethics, morals and justice seem to avoid that part of the program. There is a strong tendency in philosophy to base ethical theories on subjective intuitive data in combination with inductive reasoning, but identifying the weakness of the inductive approach so as to make it seem more valid. I think Popper made a mistake when he included the word scientific in his title translation. The *Logik der Forschung* might have been more straightforward if translated as *The Logic of Research*. Better yet, as *The Logic of Theory Formation*. Using the word scientific seems to have given permission to writers, who do not consider themselves scientists, license to reject acceptable principles of theory formation. Intellectually they know better. Knowledge is knowledge. All aspects of knowledge require proper theory formation. In the past, philosophy and science were integrated. Around the time of Hume (the patron saint of modern ethical inductive moral reasoning) and Newton (the father of Newtonian physics) philosophy and science split. We would do well to remember that the word science comes from the Latin *scire*—to know. It is not from the Latin word for test tube. Knowledge is a sphere, ever increasing in size, with a surface covered by an ever increasing number of new questions. The larger the sphere, the more the questions. Knowledge, with its covering of new questions, is broken off into what we consider bite-size chunks only for convenience. If there is to be general acceptance, all proposed theories put forth as answers to the questions, including philosophic theories, still must be managed using accepted (philosophy's own) theory formation.

We can see some common ground, some convergence, between science and philosophy expressed in quotes from physicist Lord Kelvin and philosopher Wittgenstein. In 1891 Lord Kelvin (see Andro Linklater *Measuring America*) said, "When you measure what you are speaking about, and express it in numbers, you know something about it; but when you cannot measure it, you cannot express it in numbers, your knowledge is of a meager and unsatisfactory kind." A generation later in Wittgenstein's *Tractatus* we find his famous quote, "Whereof we cannot speak, thereof we must be silent." The concept of objective data is embedded in both statements. In fact, science is the objective part of epistemology and logic. Science is merely the vernacular term for objective data and theories. Science is that part of philosophy that enables us to develop theories accepted by the group to recommend ethical behavior. While unacknowledged by Wittgenstein and many other philosophers, "natural" science is a vital, integral part of philosophy. Is there anything more natural than survival of our species? Can philosophy shut its eyes as to how we can best ensure that we accomplish this?

Here are three examples of areas of scientific research that must be considered for long-term human existence. It is my contention that these are also extremely important philosophic ethical issues and that philosophy can help advise the best way to assign assets to manage long-term versus short-term problems. First, as noted earlier, space exploration is needed to address threats from asteroids and to give us access to a second planet for human habitation. Colonization would dramatically increase our chances of perpetuation in case of catastrophe either from an asteroid or from other severe environmental degradation. Second, medical research is needed to counter continually changing infectious agents and other health threats. Note that ethically speaking, it is not necessarily important that individuals live longer and, in fact, at this point in time, longevity may be raising as many ethical problems as it solves. It is, however, important that we understand the human animal as much as possible in order to avoid disastrous effects to the species from unknown health threats in the future. Third, scientific research is needed to address environmental changes such as those caused by overpopulation and global warming—significant threats that could make it difficult or impossible to continue to live on planet earth.

These three objective threats and problems may be recognized as examples of the types of problems that require the formation of primary ethical rules. These are the problems for which theories are developed, based on objective scientific data, to determine the best way to manage the threats they represent. The developed solutions, the primary ethical rules for the group, will take precedence over the secondary ethical rules of deontology involved with group maintenance. Each of these areas involves arranging priorities and deciding how to distribute group assets. However the assets of the group are distributed, some members will benefit less and some more. If we shunt money into long-term threats by dealing with space exploration, there will be less money for the current generation, perhaps decreasing funding for the poor and needy, the less talented, the "underprivileged." If we refuse to let all members have as many children as they would like, we decrease happiness of current members. We restrict their liberty, add more rules, in order to counter the long-term threats science sees arising from overpopulation. The diseases for which we choose to increase funding will affect which patients of the current generation have the best chance of living. Still, we are forced to recognize that unlimited funding into all aspects of medicine would seriously impair funding to counter other threats. Priorities must be decided based on first countering what is most likely to be a threat to the group as a whole. Science, not metaphysics or esthetics, provides the data that permit philosophy to understand and ethically arrange these priorities.

I think philosophy let itself get seduced, and, to some extent, has restricted itself, in trying to deal with individual subjective data and theories regarding esthetics and metaphysics and the meaning of life—those things most important to the individual. Even when philosophy examines the ethics side of the structure, it has an overwhelming tendency to fall into the deontological trap of microfocusing on the secondary rules of ethics and not recognizing the overriding importance of the primary rules. I think this again, as with the use of inductive reasoning, is the result of the tradition of seeing the individual as the more important entity rather than understanding that it is the group that has priority. Philosophy needs to see the elephant whole. It can then use scientific objective data to recommend primary rules and better contribute to developing ethical conduct for humanity as a whole. Recognition of the primary rules would then permit philosophy to *objectively* integrate the secondary deontological rules into a coherent structure. By default, today ethics is handled piecemeal by politicians, lawyers, judges, economists and the military, all of whom are forced to deal with (scientific) reality without much objective practical help from philosophy.

I think it is the curse of our awareness of personal mortality that has driven us to reverse Alyosha's quote and think incorrectly that the meaning of life is more important than life. We convince ourselves to forget the basic fact that without life there is no one to question the meaning of life. We must realize that the six billion or more individual belief systems cannot take priority over perpetuation of humans. It is the blessing of our awareness that we can use an objective (scientific) philosophic approach to develop ethical behavior to delay the extinction of humans for as long as possible. That is, after all, the primary function of philosophy. It is an additional blessing that many of us can find meaning, happiness and fulfillment in our lives by working toward this goal. Awareness can thus let us see our transient existence not as trivial and condemned by Pascal's chain, but as the forgers of our generation's important link in the chain of human existence. It is my fervent hope that we might do this job so well, ethically speaking, that we can give this same opportunity to our collective grandchildren's grandchildren and their children and grandchildren so they each may have the pleasure and happiness of individually pondering the existential meaning of life.

APPENDIX

THE FUNCTIONAL APPLICATION OF THE ELEMENTS OF PHILOSOPHY

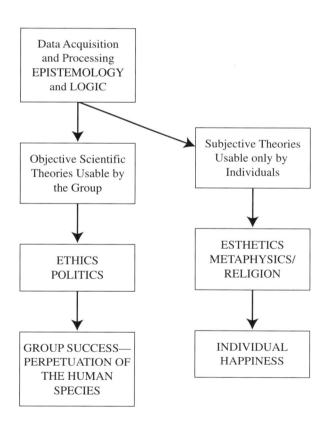

MUTUAL OBLIGATIONS AND ADVANTAGES INVOLVED IN DEONTOLOGICAL CONTRACTS BETWEEN THE GROUP AND ITS INDIVIDUAL MEMBERS

Group's Obligations*
Individuals' Advantages

1) Protection
2) Equal Opportunity
3) Noninterference with the individual's pursuit of happiness

Individuals' Obligations

1) Acknowledge the primacy of the group's primary goal
   a) The group's goal of perpetuation always takes precedence over the individual's secondary goal—particularly the pursuit of happiness.
   b) The individual conducts himself or herself in a manner to ensure that the group's goal will be accomplished. This includes following the written rules of the group, but conduct needed to maximize chances to accomplish the goal is not restricted to the written rules†.

---

* These obligations as well as the obligations of the individual members below can also be referred to as the secondary ethical rules since fulfillment can be preempted in times of group need, if justified, ethically speaking, by the exigencies of the primary goal and the primary rules.

† Many of the unwritten rules involve the secondary ethical rules required for group maintenance and deal with how other members of the group must be treated and include the virtues, do-unto-others, etc. Deontologically speaking, they primarily represent part of the contract with the group, not a contract with other individuals in the group. Doing the "right thing," including correct treatment of other individuals in the group, is an obligation owed the group and assumed because it is necessary to achieve the group's primary goal.

Advantages for the Larger Group

1) Assuming adequate resources, increased number of members permits:
    a) Increased capability of protection
    b) Increased talent available to the group
    c) Increased genetic possibilities
    d) Increased specialization to handle a wider variety of threats

SUMMARY

The end product of philosophy is to recommend appropriate conduct—how we should live. Philosophy does this by recognizing that all humans have two goals. First, as members of humanity we have a part in helping the group achieve perpetuation of the human species. Second, as individual human beings, we pursue the goal of happiness. (Happiness is used as an umbrella term encompassing contentment, satisfaction, self-fulfillment, etc.) For philosophy to offer any consistent, useful advice regarding conduct, it must prioritize between these two goals. The assumption of this book is that perpetuation of the species is the more important goal. With this prioritization used as an objective frame of reference, this book develops a functional organization and structure of philosophy. Philosophy advises conduct that will provide the maximum happiness for each generation of individuals (the secondary goal considered in esthetics and metaphysics) consistent with not impairing the ability of humanity as a whole in its effort to perpetuate the species (the primary goal considered in ethics and politics).

The conduct for achieving these intertwined but prioritized goals is determined through the process of acquiring data and using this data to develop predictive, cause-and-effect theories (epistemology and logic). Based on these resultant theories, conduct can then be recommended. The data and theories are of two types: objective and subjective. Objective (scientific) is defined as that capable of being accepted by other members of the human group who are both disinterested and knowledgeable. Subjective is defined as that which is acceptable to some individuals but not capable of being agreed upon by disinterested and knowledgeable other members of the group as a whole. Theories formed to recommend group conduct (ethics) for achieving the primary goal require group agreement and thus require the use of objective data to produce objective theories. Theories formed by individuals in the pursuit of happiness (esthetics and metaphysics—primarily religion) need to convince only the individuals involved of their usefulness and can therefore use subjective as well as objective data to develop subjective theories.

Conduct is the means whereby the two human goals are accomplished. Only a group can accomplish perpetuation. Conduct that contributes to giving the group the best chance of perpetuating the species is defined as ethical. Objective ethical theories are necessarily changed as new or improved data become available and as new threats or changes in resources demand. Changes in objective theories will thus result in ever-changing recommended ethical conduct. Humans must form groups in order to accomplish perpetuation. Deontology is the obligations and advantages agreed to between the group as a whole and its individual members that permit the formation, maintenance and efficient functioning of the group. The group's obligations to its individual members are providing protection, providing equal opportunity and permitting group members to pursue happiness. The individual members' obligation is to always act in such a manner that will permit the group to have the best chance of perpetuating itself. The group's need of perpetuation takes precedence over all other obligations. Thus, the restriction on the pursuit of individual happiness (and on any of the other obligations in the deontological contract) is that *it cannot be ethically permitted if so doing would impair the group's ability to achieve the primary goal.* The *bête-noire* of ethics, however, is the tendency of individuals to continue to pursue their own happiness even if it is detrimental to the more important primary goal of the group.

INDEX

abortion, 113–15
absolute truth, 23
Adams, John, 27, 105
adjustable ethics, 63
advantage(s)
    chosen for human race survival, 92
    and environmental protection, 118, 119
    and equal opportunity, 100, 101, 102
    of group membership, 32, 37, 48, 54, 56–57, 73
    of group mergers, 39, 40–41
    and group obligations, 43–44, 46, 56–57, 136
    of individual group members, 34, 35–36, 85, 136
    of orators, 68
    of religion, 80, 97
    of slave ownership, 104, 105, 106, 108
    and unequal accumulation of group assets, 29
    of world groups, 49–52
Alyosha, 9, 74, 134
America. *See* United States of America
The Analects of Confucius (Leys), 17, 128
animals
    position vs. humans, 14, 15, 31–32, 87, 93
    survival-of-the-fittest method of species perpetuation, 28
Arab Americans, 93
Arabs, 126–27
Archimedean point, 16
Aristotle, 9, 10, 12, 27, 104
Armstrong, Karen, 97
Aurelius, Marcus, 17, 34
awareness, 15, 28, 48, 57, 134

Bacharach, Burt, 123
Bible, 1, 124, 125
birth control, 54, 73, 79, 113–15
Buddha, 30

Cahill, Thomas, 38
Calicles, 30
Casablanca, 61
China, 21, 69, 79, 114
Christ, 1, 30, 33, 124
Christianity, 40, 69, 80, 97, 124–25
Churchill, Winston, 95
Civil War, 105–6, 109
communication, 37, 48, 49, 97
conduct, 138
Confucius, 5, 17, 129
consequence(s)
    ethical considerations, 35, 41, 48, 54, 58, 78, 121
    of group goals, 29
    of justice, 85

of slavery, 105
of suicide, 110, 112
of war, 96
Constitution of the United States of America, 44–46, 105, 109
contracts, 28. *See also* deontological contracts

Darwin, Charles, 48, 95, 130
David, Hal, 123
death penalty, 112–13
decadence, 71–73, 128
Declaration of Independence, 45
deductive reasoning and theory, 17, 59–61, 88, 91
Democrats, 36, 117
deontological contracts
　Declaration of Independence, 45
　Jews in Nazi Germany, 125, 126
　obligations and advantages, 44, 136
　parties involved in, 46
　secondary ethical values, 55–56
　slavery issues, 107, 108
　U.S. Constitution, 45
　world group formation, 49
deontology, 37, 50, 133, 138
Descartes, René, 130
dinosaurs, 119, 120
Discourses (Machiavelli), 128
Dostoyevsky, Fyodor, 9
do-unto-others, 46, 49, 57, 58
Durant, Ariel, 2, 128
Durant, Will, 2, 128

education, 36, 106, 107, 108, 129
ego, 30
egoless system, 30
Einstein, Albert, 19, 20, 67, 68
The Elements of Moral Philosophy (Rachels), 81
empirical knowledge, 20
environment
　ethics regarding, 55, 78, 116–19
　preservation of, 15, 93
　threats to, 50, 58, 63

epistemology, defined, 17–18
Epstein, Julius, 61
Epstein, Philip, 61
equality of opportunity
　African Americans, 107
　definition of, 99
　as group obligation, 136
　importance of, 31, 99–100
　in Nazi Germany, 125
　vs. equality of value, 30
　women, 99–103
equality of value, 30–31, 99
equality of women, 99–103
Eskimos, 82, 86, 115
esthetics, 20, 65–69
ethical conduct, definition of, 4
ethical egoism, 61
ethical rules, primary, 56–57, 78–79, 116, 133
ethical rules, secondary. *See* secondary ethical rules
ethical systems, 28–29, 33–34, 57–59, 63, 83, 117
ethical war, 94–96
ethics
　definition of, 2, 4, 10
　vs. morals, 77–89
evil
　Nietzsche on, 77, 130
　religious forces, 120
　on unethical scale, 47, 71, 126–27
evolution, 13, 14, 24
existentialism, 18, 74, 134

falsifiable data, 21, 40, 80, 83
falsifiable values, 11
Foot, Philippa, 130
fractal quality, of groups, 49

genetic diversity, 92, 98, 125
genocide, 98
Germany, 33, 125–26
global warming, 118, 132
goals, 10–11

God
  belief in, 69
  in Declaration of Independence, 54
  ethics specification, 62, 80
  existence of, 20–21
  in U.S. Constitution, 44
  war images of, 97
good, greatest, 3, 10–16, 47, 60, 66, 75, 121
government, 43
A History of God (Armstrong), 97
A History of Western Philosophy (Russell), 9, 60, 104, 127

Hobbes, Thomas, 38
Hobson's choice, 105
Holocaust, 1, 68, 124–27
How the Irish Saved Civilization (Cahill), 38
Hume, David, 59, 131

inductive reasoning and theory, 59–60, 87, 130, 131, 133
infanticide, 82, 86, 115
intuition, 83

Jefferson, Thomas, 45, 105
Jesus Christ, 1, 30, 33, 124
Jews, 97, 124–27
Jonestown, 16
justice
  and death penalty, 112–13
  Kant on, 4, 88
  as moral theory, 83–86, 95, 126
  slavery, 103
  and suicide, 110–11
  U.S. Constitution, 44
  as virtue, 94
just war, 94–96

Kant, Immanuel, 4, 30, 58, 83
Kelvin, Lord William Thomson, 131–32
Kierkegaard, Soren, 74
Koch, Howard, 61
Koran, 104

Larsen, Edward, 69
Lee, Harper, 72
Leys, Simon, 17
liberty
  definition of, 5
  and environmentalism, 117
  and population control, 133
  and property ownership, 116
  and slavery, 104
  vs. equality, 29–36, 68, 87, 124, 128, 130
  and war, 99, 117
  and world groups, 51
lifeboat, 91–92, 115, 116
Lincoln, Abraham, 105, 128
Linklater, Andro, 132
Lucretius, 120

Machiavelli, Niccolo, 41, 59, 87, 91, 94, 128
Mars, 119
Marx, Karl, 75
Maslow, Abraham, 70
materialism, 72, 73
maudism, 72, 73
maximizing notion, 84
McCarthy, Joseph, 48
McCullough, David, 27
metaphysics, definition of, 68–69
Montesquieu, 77
morals
  evolution of, 130
  vs. ethics, 77–89
More, Thomas, 85
Mutually Assured Destruction (MAD), 62, 126

nation, 48
Natural Goodness (Foot), 130
Nazi Germany, 33, 125–26
Neanderthals, 48
Nietzsche, Friedrich, 1, 14, 30, 33, 36, 77, 124, 130
nonempirical, 68
nonviolence, 73, 99

nuclear war, 55, 126
nuclear weapons, 16, 50, 62, 116

objective data and theories, 18–25
   definition of, 138
   See also secular world
objective truth, 9, 16, 121
obligation(s)
   Constitutional obligations, 44–45, 46, 109
   of equal opportunity and protection, 107, 125
   ethical exceptions to, 75
   ethical/unethical actions regarding, 43–44, 46–47, 54
   of group, 56, 100, 136, 138
   in group formation, 37, 40, 41
   and Holocaust, 125, 126
   individuals within group, 110, 136, 138
   justice as, 84, 86
   perpetuation of group as most important, 138
   and slavery issue, 106, 107, 108
   and suicide, 110
   in world group formation, 49, 50, 51, 52
one-world group, 49–52, 57

Palestinians, 111–12
Pascal, Blaise, 69–70, 134
perpetuation of species
   as ethical theory, 121
   as most important function, 13–16
philosophy
   conduct recommendations, 137–38
   flow chart of elements of, 135
   functional definition of, 4–5
Plato, 30, 34, 60, 104
politics, definition of, 29
Popper, Karl, 1, 123
primary ethical rules, 56–57, 78–79, 116, 133
The Prince (Machiavelli), 91, 128

The Principles of Ethics (Spencer), 27, 130
promises
   breaking/keeping of, 41, 56, 59–60, 94, 128
   between individual members of group, 46
   of U.S. Constitution, 44
property, 104, 116, 117

Quisling, Vidkun, 48
Qur'an, 104

Rachels, James, 81, 82
Rand, Ayn, 35
Rawls, John, 83, 84, 85, 86
reason, 57, 74
relativism, 81–82
religion
   decadence, 71, 72–73
   divisiveness of, 120–21
   and ethical system establishment, 53–55, 62
   goodness of, 75
   historical role of, 128
   importance of, 81
   of individual and subordination to group goals, 6, 39, 40, 74
   mass suicide inspired by, 16
   and metaphysics, 69–70
   and morals, 79–81, 82
   as "opiate of masses," 74–75
   subjectivity of, 11, 87, 93
   U.S. Constitution on, 44–45
   and war, 96–98
   and world group membership, 52
   and wrongness of Holocaust, 1, 124–25
Republicans, 36, 117
Republic (Plato), 30
Russell, Bertrand, 9, 11, 16, 60, 104, 121, 127

Sandburg, Carl, 128
Santayana, George, 65

Sartre, Jean Paul, 74
Scanlon, T. M., 46
secondary ethical rules
  basis for, 55–57
  benefits of, 94
  and customs, 82
  and justice, 84
  primary ethical rules' priority over, 133
  stability of, 78
secular countries, 52
secular world
  changes to, 96–97
  concept of vs. subjective, 11, 12
  decadent excesses of, 72
  elimination of by religious people, 120–21
  goals of, 12–16
  perpetuation of species, 28, 53
  political/governmental structures, 53–54
  population control, 114
  precedence over subjective, 24, 72
  and religious rules, 54–55, 74–75
  war, 98
self-preservation, 13, 62
Shinto, 130
slavery, 103–10
space station, 92
Spencer, Herbert, 27, 48, 95, 130
Spinoza, Baruch, 13, 62
subjective data and theories, 18, 20–24
  definition of, 138
  See also supernatural world
suicide, 16, 110–12, 127
suicide bombings, 111–12, 127
supernatural policeman, 54, 80
supernatural world
  beliefs and faith regarding, 74
  concept of vs. objective, 11
  danger of, 23–24
  and ethics, 62
  goals of, 11–12, 16
  happiness, 68, 69
  and morals, 80
  as synonym for metaphysics, 69
  truth, 119
  See also religion
survival-of-the-fittest
  Darwin/Spencer on, 48–49, 95
  definition of, 28
  faith-based continuation of, 62
  origination of, 130
  and slavery, 104
  theory of, 15
  war, 50, 98

Tattersall, Ian, 48
teleology, 23
testability
  ethical theories, 78, 83
  existence of God, 21
  moral goals, 88
  objective theories, 19, 78
  politics, 29, 131
  subjective theories, 22–24
  theories, generally, 131
Their Finest Hour (Churchill), 95
theocracy, 53–54
To Kill a Mockingbird (Lee), 72
truth
  absolute truth, 23
  Declaration of Independence on, 45
  individual vs. group, 119–20
  Kierkegaard on, 74
  objective truth, 9, 16, 121
  personal truth, 99
  religious beliefs, 80, 96–97
  subjective approaches to, 23–24
  universal truth, 82

unethical conduct, definition of, 4
United States of America
  concept of God, 21, 69
  Constitution of, 44–46, 105, 109
  death penalty, 113

Declaration of Independence, 45
environmental issues, 118
ethnic identity, 93
political systems, 36
population control, 114
role of government, 42
slavery in, 103–10
unethical politicians, 48
war, 99
world group role, 50–51
universal truth, 82
utilitarianism, 6
utilitarian theories, 88
Utopia (More), 85

variables, in ethical systems, 57–58
verifiability
    existence of God, 21, 69
    intuitive data, 83
    objective data, 18
    subjective goals/data, 16, 20, 80
    theories, 19
    values, 11
    world's goal, 63, 80

virtues
    Confucian, 78
    ethical considerations, 46, 59, 119
    and goal prioritization, 10
    and group functioning, 56, 94
    justice as, 84
    Spinoza on, 13, 62

war
    analogy to justice and punishment, 113
    Civil War, 105–6, 109
    ethical considerations, 62, 94–99, 119
    individual pursuits during, 71
    ineffectiveness of, 50–51
    liberty-equality spectrum, 117–18
    religious-based, 55
Williams, Bernard, 2
Winik, Jay, 105
Witham, Larry, 69
Wittgenstein, Ludwig, 131
world group, 49–52, 57